AND

PUBLIC SPEAKING

NEIL GUNTHER

DAVID & CHARLES
Newton Abbot   London

First published in Australia by Reed Books Pty Ltd, 1980
Revised edition by Reed Books Pty Ltd, 1986
First published in Great Britain by David & Charles Publishers plc, 1987

British Library Cataloguing in Publication Data

Gunther, Neil
   Debating and public speaking: how to
   speak and argue effectively.
   1. Public speaking
   I. Title
   808.5'1   PN4121

   ISBN 0-7153-9015-5

Printed in Great Britain
by Billings Limited, Worcester
for David & Charles Publishers plc
Brunel House   Newton Abbot   Devon

Contents

Foreword

Means of verbal communication have moved a long way since the days when people could communicate with other people only when they were face-to-face. Even so, getting in touch through television, radio, telephone, and other such systems is still basically speaking and listening. If our verbal communication is to be effective it is important that each person should possess keenly-developed speaking and listening ability. Debating and public speaking provide opportunities for this skill to be practised and extended.

Neil Gunther is well qualified to present a thoroughly practical explanation of how to speak and argue effectively. As teacher, speaker, debater, coach, adjudicator, he has demonstrated his mastery of the techniques he writes about. As the first Organiser of Debating, NSW Department of Education, his research into all aspects of speaking and debating, coupled with his wide experience of coaching outstanding debaters, has equipped him to establish a number of new and highly-successful approaches which are described in these pages. He has pioneered instructional classes in debating and established Australia's only training course for adjudicators.

This book covers a wide field with insight, precision, and style. It should find ready acceptance in debating circles, among public-speaking groups, in staff development schemes, in the classroom, and in the broader fields of education. Libraries should welcome such an authoritative addition to works on verbal communication. People, at whatever stage of speaking skill, should be both challenged and assisted when using this book. It may be expected to serve as the major handbook on debating and public speaking for many years.

Noel H. Cislowski
Member of Board of Directors
City of Sydney Cultural Council

Preface to Third Impression

Since publication of the second impression, the public-speaking material contained in Chapters 2-3 has appeared in considerably expanded form in my book "The Art of Effective Speaking" (Reed Books, 1982).

The opportunity has been taken to increase the number of subjects for debate (Chapter 9) from 200 to 700. The new subjects are numbered 201-700.

N.G.

CHAPTER ONE

The Twofold Lively Art

Speaking and arguing effectively

Think, speak, put a point of view, argue that view against a conflicting view, convince people that we have won the argument. That's what most of us do, or try to do, for much of the time. Some do it effectively, but most do not. And the basic reasons for not speaking and arguing effectively are lack of precise knowledge of how to go about it and lack of practice in doing it.

Thinking, unless we aim to live in the silent world of our own thoughts, must be given expression, and that is done in the first place through speaking. Speech is the simplest and commonest form of communication. But its simplicity is deceptive. To communicate through speech requires the ability to speak clearly, intelligibly, and in such a way as to secure attention.

Speaking effectively shouldn't be seen merely as a matter of talking to just a few people. As the numbers increase from a handful to twenty, fifty, a hundred, effective communication becomes a greater challenge. It's therefore advisable to be able to command the attention of a larger audience in order to develop an assurance of being in reasonable command of any speaking situation which may arise.

Public speaking, with its extension in the form of debating, is one of the lively arts, together with such others as music, theatre, and ballet. People who have seen and heard skilled speakers and debaters in action are well aware of the strong, exciting appeal they make. To take part in, or just to be present at, a debating battle of wits, where the intellect, personality, and linguistic verve of the two teams are blended in a sparkling pattern of communication and disputation, is something to remember. And it's only a little less absorbing to be involved in a public-speaking performance where the audience can be persuaded to hang on every word.

This book has three objects:
- to compare the advantages of public speaking and debating as two forms of the art of spoken communication (Chapter 1);
- to explain the techniques of public speaking (Chapters 2-3);
- to explain the techniques of debating, training of debaters, and adjudication of debates (Chapters 4-8). An extended treatment

of these is given on account of the large number of issues involved.

Debaters are particularly reminded that, as many things which apply to debating apply in the first instance to public speaking, Chapters 2-3, "Background to Public Speaking" and "How to Use Your Voice", should be studied before the debating section is read. Manner, for example, is almost wholly covered in Chapter 2, and the general aspects of matter and method are also dealt with in that chapter.

Public speaking and debating: similarities and differences

Both public speaking and debating depend for effectiveness on the ability to capture and hold audience attention. An important aspect of both is manner, which may be described briefly as how the voice is produced and employed, the choice of language, and the expression of personality, or in summary as the style of spoken communication. Just as a public speaker must have a subject to give purpose to his manner, so must a debater. The public speaker is required to organise his thoughts in order to present them coherently and fit them to the subject, and the debater is required to do this and, in addition, to fit them to a line of argument.

Whereas the public speaker's concern may be to express a point of view, to state and elaborate a theme, he is often concerned simply to inform or perhaps to present a mixture of information and entertainment; but the debater, though he may be concerned to some extent to inform and entertain, is essentially in the business of arguing a point of view with the object of gaining support for it, and of refuting an opposing point of view. The public speaker's concern is communication, but the debater's concern is communication and conflict.

It has sometimes been said, by persons who don't know what they're talking about (or by failed debaters), that debating is too artificial an exercise to be undertaken by public speakers. But it's such a valuable and challenging exercise that public speakers should take it up at the first opportunity. It's particularly rewarding in that it offers in an intellectual sphere the fascination of combat, between individuals or teams, according to the type of debate. It may be described as the next step for the public speaker who wishes to change from a solo performance, brilliant as it may sometimes be, to a more complex one in which his skills are pitted against those of other speakers.

Debaters, likewise, should accept that they have much to learn from public speaking, for the essentials of communication, being the framework on which argument is built, necessarily precede the argument. And if they concentrate on combat to the exclusion of the graces which form part of a successful public speaker's equipment they are likely to find that audiences, which are always prepared to be captivated by manner, receive them without much warmth.

An important feature of both public speaking and debating is the part they play in creating and maintaining confidence, that quality so necessary to everyone who wishes to feel at ease among his fellows. There are doubtless other ways of gaining it, but the serious drawback to some of them is the ease with which they may lead to the unlovely attributes of brashness and over-confidence. Public speakers and debaters who allow themselves to develop these qualities invariably find that audience toleration of them is short, and so the public speaking and debating situation of itself cures the normally unwanted excesses of the attributes it develops.

Many situations in life require us to display courage before other people and to communicate effectively with them. We don't succeed in this accidentally, but through having had some experience in the matter. Perhaps the best way of gaining this experience is by speaking in public. He who has learnt to be at ease in speaking to an audience will be equally so in a variety of situations, where communication is an important factor, whether it be attending an employment interview, putting a case to some authority for consideration, or even explaining the advantages of a course of action to people.

Special advantages of debating

Debating promotes certain valuable skills above those obtainable from public speaking. It requires the following:
* choice of a particular theme or line to support an argument;
* organisation of ideas to develop that line;
* development of ideas to refute an opposing argument, and of further ideas to reinforce the original one;
* clear and effective expression of both sets of ideas;
* ability to argue logically and persuasively;
* marshalling of evidence in support of argument;
* intellectual teamwork.

The last two of these skills deserve special comment. The requirement of evidence means that debaters need to be aware not merely of recognised ways of making their arguments appear reasonable, but of the various errors of reasoning. Intellectual teamwork, the working together to achieve a common end, is important in any intellectual activity where resources must be pooled for a common benefit. Debates are not won by speakers, no matter how brilliant, who neglect to combine their skills with those of their colleagues for mutual advantage. And they're not won by any speaker whose notion of co-operation is of something extended to him by others, never the other way round. Team debating therefore has positive social value.

An important social benefit provided by debating concerns the use of an audience. It's fundamental to a debate that the two teams should endeavour to convince a body of people of the relative merits of the cases being argued. Contact must be made and held with the audience, for without audience response the debaters may well find their confidence vanishing in a cloud of artificiality. In fact, if for some reason a debate has to take place without an audience the teams need to be adept at filling the empty seats with imaginary people on whom to practise the arts of persuasion. With audience response, which debaters must create for themselves, they can maintain and often improve their levels of performance. To give this response the audience is drawn into the debate as into any other cultural happening, becomes part of the event, and gains from watching and listening in like measure as each team gains from trying to convince the audience.

Debating is independent of age or sex. Upper primary pupils can be successfully initiated into it, as can mentally alert senior citizens. An accomplished debater in, say, the sixteen to nineteen years of age group is likely to be a most worthy opponent, with such concentration and persuasive sincerity as some of his elders may have forgotten existed, and there can never be any certainty that capable older teams will defeat capable younger ones. Debating seems to be particularly suited to persons of mature intellect and outgoing personality, of whatever age. If the intellect lacks some maturity at the outset, hard debating often hastens the maturing process.

Though debating is an intellectual activity, it isn't something purely for intellectuals. Certainly dumb blondes and all-in wrestlers don't make a success of it, but they rarely succeed at anything except being themselves. Ordinary folk do well at debating, as at most things, once they've mastered the technique. In fact, a noticeable proportion of competent debaters consists of persons who recognise their limitations but employ sound technique and make full use of conflict. It's agreeable to record that teams of such debaters gain a share of their wins against teams of intellectuals who sometimes can't resist the temptation to sheer off at a mind-bending tangent.

Australian debating style

This is of particular importance. Australian debating seems to differ strongly from that of other English-speaking countries (except New Zealand, where, however, audience interjections are permitted) in being essentially a combination of communication and conflict, with the latter as the fundamental feature for which the former provides the channel. Any debating book which fails to stress the need to frame the fight to suit the developing occasion will be of little help.

The communication-conflict style of debating has long been accepted by the Australian Debating Federation and the State Debating unions which are its member bodies, and is the basis on which performances are assessed at the two annual national carnivals, for State representative adults' and school students' teams respectively. Consequently it's the accepted style for all competition debating in this country, from school to adult levels. The Australian context is an integral part of this book.

Understanding techniques

Though a remarkable surge of interest in spoken communication in Australia has been obvious since the mid-1970s, as shown by a sharp increase in the number of schools taking part in public speaking and debating competitions, and the emergence and growing popularity of schools' State-wide and Australia-wide contests in both fields, a sound knowledge of essential techniques has lagged behind.

Of the large numbers of people who take part in sport or watch it, most know the rules of whatever game interests them and what techniques are suited to common situations. Yet, of the considerable numbers who take part in or watch debates, though most know what's permitted and what isn't, relatively few understand the techniques of conflict, the means by which advantage may be gained or offset. Yet this, once the idea of communication has been grasped, is what debating is all about.

Many public speakers don't know how to select and organise their material to the best advantage or how to communicate effectively. Many of their listeners, lacking sufficient knowledge of the special skills by which speakers should seek to create necessary impact, are unable to follow their speeches with a proper sense of critical appreciation, and this means that they're not sufficiently equipped to respond with the degree of warmth needed to allow speakers to gain assurance and raise their level of performance.

Public speakers, debaters, and their audiences all require an explanation of the basic techniques of public speaking and debating. Competitive speakers need to remember that the correct application of these techniques often makes the difference between winning and losing, and always makes the difference between experiencing a sense of satisfaction and one of disappointment that somewhere a wrong turning must have been taken. Audiences need to be reminded that enjoyment of any kind of performance depends on knowing just what the participants are, or should be, trying to do and on being able to judge the result.

It may not be so obvious that there's need for explanation of how to coach public speakers and debaters so that they can reach and maintain whatever level of performance can fairly be expected of them, and that there's a particular need to explain the principles of adjudication and training of adjudicators.

Learning by doing is a necessary process, but it should be undertaken as a follow-up to specific instruction and not be carried out on a trial-and-error basis at the possible expense of those on whom it's practised. Training of adjudicators and adjudication of debates are specialised tasks requiring provision of information on how to go about them. This is especially necessary in the case of adjudication, which is an end-process. Public speakers and debaters may succeed despite indifferent coaching, if they have the ability to learn for themselves, but their progress may well be halted by indifferent adjudication.

Adjudicators of considerable experience and sound judgment maintain high standards, as should be expected, and those who have satisfactorily completed a well-planned course of instruction may be depended on to give informed and acceptable decisions. However, many adjudicators don't happen to fall within those two groups, and their decisions are likely to be of the hit-or-miss variety. And there's no doubt that well-meaning adjudicators of doubtful competence hinder development of the art of spoken communication when they give verdicts which are open to serious question or which, even though apparently correct, are not supported by clear and firm reasons.

The need to train adjudicators, or at least to supply them with a fairly comprehensive set of instructions which they could follow in regions where the establishment of a course of instruction presented some difficulty, was realised by the New South Wales Department of Education in the late 1970s as the number of teams in its competitions, which had been growing steadily, eased to a gentle gradient after passing 750. An increasing incidence of unsatisfactory decisions dictated abandonment of a long-standing but never really defensible tradition that adjudicators need only be professional persons, clergymen, housewives, ex-teachers, people of some community standing, or those with some present or past debating experience. It was even found that interstate debaters were not necessarily competent judges of the art they practised with some distinction.

A training course for prospective adjudicators was therefore established, and no new adjudicator is now appointed in the Sydney region unless he has completed it satisfactorily. Existing adjudicators are required to keep abreast of developments by attending an annual meeting at which they mark a debate and take part in discussion. A set of instructions is issued to adjudicators who, because they work in country districts, are unable to attend the course in Sydney.

What this adds up to is that adjudicators don't just happen to pick up correct techniques and standards of judgment, but require instruction. At the time of writing, oddly enough, no training course for them exists in Australia apart from the one conducted in Sydney for a limited number of invited applicants. It would do a great deal for debating and public speaking if such courses could be held in cities and country areas in all States. However, they take time and money to arrange and hold, and there's the problem of getting enough qualified persons to conduct them.

Clearly the first step must be to provide the means for interested persons to read details of the principles and specialised techniques of adjudication.

CHAPTER TWO
Background To Public Speaking

Basic features

There are three types of speeches: prepared, impromptu, and instant. Prepared and impromptu speeches are recognised for competition purposes, while instant speeches, as in debating, are valuable as aids to training and as exhibition items. Most public speaking, of course, isn't concerned with competitions, and speeches are then the result of varying degrees of preparation. Effective speeches, however, need to have an impromptu quality, in that they should sound very much as if the speaker were making up his remarks as he goes. Speeches which lack this quality are in danger of descending to the depths of prepared statements, things from which humanity and warmth have been intentionally but misguidedly removed.

A speech of any type has in essence one or more of three objects: to inform, argue a point of view, or entertain. Experienced speakers usually season argument with information, not simply to give it necessary support but to avoid creating an impression of forcing their own opinions on people. Where entertainment isn't the prime object, and except on the most serious occasions, speakers who wish to hold audience interest normally add a dash of it in the form of light touches.

In competitions a prepared speech is usually on a set or pre-arranged subject, though sometimes the speaker may choose it himself, and preparation time is unlimited. An impromptu speech, which was often considered a remarkable feat when instant speeches were unheard of, is governed by the limitations that the subject is revealed, and preparation begins, some two or three minutes before speaking time, usually just as the previous speaker gets under way. An instant speech is given with no preparation, the subject being announced at the moment the speaker is called on. Standard meeting procedure is followed with all speeches, in that there is a chairman, who introduces speaker and subject, is addressed by the speaker to begin with, and keeps time. And there's an adjudicator.

In marking speeches, the adjudicator normally follows debating practice in taking account of matter, manner, and method to fix a

40-40-20-100 maximum, but with those speeches, especially of impromptu type, which last only a few minutes it's common merely to award the total mark. A popular notion that manner is virtually supreme in competitive public speaking is false, for the content and organisation of a speech cannot be ignored. Shortage of material may lose as many marks as are gained by impressive manner, and method marks will suffer if matter is poorly arranged, as is the case when time and emphasis are not well distributed. Use of time, in fact, is more critical than in debating because, there being no need for extended development or for refutation of an opposing case, a speaker is only allowed about two-thirds of the time of a debater in a competition of similar standard.

Though there are numbers of speakers in a competition, each speaks for himself and is judged on an individual performance in relation to other individual performances. This frees him from the excitement and tension of close combat, and allows him to present himself simply as someone with something to say which he proposes to say in his own distinctive fashion.

The approach to public speaking should be the same, whatever the occasion. It may be the case of a director addressing a board meeting, a union leader addressing delegates, an executive speaking to his subordinates, a lecturer informing an audience, an after-dinner speaker endeavouring to say nothing of much consequence but to say it wittily, someone who has caught the chairman's eye at a meeting, a school student criticising an interpretation in literature or history, a political candidate giving a speech before a selection committee, or a competitor in a public speaking contest. If the speech is to be successful, various requirements must be met.

Obviously a speaker must know how to use his voice, but that raises so many matters as to deserve a chapter to itself (Chapter 3). What's needed at this point is an explanation of the roles of matter, manner, and method in a public speech. Manner is the same in public speaking and debating, but matter and method show certain differences in the two forms of communication.

Matter is the content of a speech, how it would appear if written out. Manner is the way in which the speaker presents his material. Method is how the material is organised, and covers basic structure of the speech, orderly progression of ideas, and allotment of time to each item in proportion to the importance being attached to it. Matter and method are closely connected, and, although poor matter isn't likely to be redeemed by sound method, useful matter loses much of its appeal when poorly arranged.

Matter and preparation

Before a speech can be given it usually has to be prepared. An expert in a particular field, who is used to talking about it, may find preparation unnecessary and acquire a pleasant informality by making up his speech as he goes along. When, as in most cases, there is preparation, it should be governed by the occasion, the expected audience, and the amount of time set aside for it. There should never be over-preparation, as this promotes the error of rushing through material and so preventing proper appreciation of its worth. Under-preparation doesn't matter if the speaker has enough knowledge of his subject to expand his material on the spot or to illustrate points at somewhat greater length.

Preparation begins, as in debating, with any necessary definition and interpretation of the subject, so that it will be clear what the theme of the speech is, what is to be covered, and in what way. Once the chief points have been decided, the treatment of them should be worked out and illustrations planned. Thought is worth giving to the beginning, ending, and intermediate highlights. Telling phrases and sentences repay time spent in devising them. Generally it's better to make notes as a help to preparation than to write out the speech (unless copies are to be distributed for information or publication), for when it's all set down beforehand the speaker may be tempted into various errors. He may learn it (or most of it) and lose spontaneity in delivering it, he may become so familiar with the written words as to give the impression of having learnt it and thereby lose freshness of contact with the audience, he may bring it with him and lose contact by consulting it too frequently, or he may read it aloud and so fail to make any contact.

In the speech itself it's wise to resist any tendency to go into considerable detail on some point, for most of it won't be remembered; to use quotations other than sparsely, for people would prefer to know your thoughts than to know you've copied someone else's (which may be hackneyed or of doubtful value, anyway); to relate lengthy anecdotes, which waste precious time and often have a poor connection with the rest of the speech; and to drag in humour, other than light touches, if it doesn't really belong there, in the vain hope that the audience will accept second-rate matter because it's seasoned with a joke.

It's sometimes claimed that the matter of a speech can itself be dull. That's most unlikely to be true unless its content is largely technical, in which case it shouldn't be given before a general audience. Non-technical matter, or matter for which technical details merely provide a background, can be made interesting to ordinary audiences by proper selection of material and such use of illustration as will relate the material to common experience. Then, of course, how the material is presented is of great importance. In a speech this is a question of the speaker's manner.

Manner is the personal quality employed by a speaker to win and hold audience appeal. It has many component parts, but all combine to make up the way in which he communicates his personality.

Manner

The parts of manner are as follows:
- eye contact with the audience;
- limited or no use of notes;
- use of good conversational English;
- clear articulation and proper voice projection;
- variation in vocal pitch, pace, tone, and volume, with planned use of pause;
- pleasing deportment;
- use of natural and unobtrusive gesture;
- projection of a satisfying personality.

These are covered below with the exception of the two items on voice production, which are more fittingly treated in Chapter 3, "How to Use Your Voice".

Eye contact with the audience must be maintained throughout the speech, for there's no hope of commanding the attention of people without looking at them, and as far as possible at each one of them as individuals rather than as members of an amorphous mass. The faces of the audience are the speaker's barometer. Looking into a person's eyes normally produces a reaction, however slight, and if it's one of interest, as it should be, his confidence is heightened and with it his level of performance. This reaction won't be forthcoming if he gives the impression that his listeners are not sufficiently important to be looked at while he's speaking to them.

Dependence on notes is a thing of the past, although public speakers who haven't been exposed to the thrust of modern debating competitions may not realise this. Looking at notes and looking at the audience are mutually exclusive, and it's the audience which counts. Notes cannot boost a speaker's confidence through favourable reaction any more than can such other favourite targets of many speakers' eyes as the ceiling, the walls, the scene outside the window, or the floor in front of the first row of seats. Notes can create the impression that the speaker needs a crutch to help him along, that what he's saying isn't part of him, but something of which he isn't very sure.

Many competent speakers refuse to use notes, even when giving an address lasting a half-hour or more. Some school student speakers leave their notes on the table when they stand up, while most others with even moderate experience carry notes unobtrusively and glance at them infrequently. That's the only way for a speaker to handle them if he feels they're necessary. But he should ask himself just how far they are necessary. In most speeches it's the quality, not the quantity, of what's said that matters. Too much in this instance not only spoils the flavour but is likely to give the audience indigestion. It's better for the speaker to cover only a few items but to cover them with the directness and sincerity which can spring so largely from making up the words as he goes.

If a speaker prefers to have his notes with him (even if only to occupy his left hand while he gestures with his right), he should know what kind of notes to have and how to manage them. Basic points and occasional catchlines are best set in large writing on small cards which can be fitted in the palm of the hand so that they're scarcely visible from the front. With practice such cards may be shuffled during a speech without attracting attention. Sheets of paper are out because they can't be concealed, and a speaker's appeal plummets when his lack of expertise is obvious. And it isn't a matter of hoping to conceal them by placing them on a lectern, for no self-respecting speaker would permit such an object to separate him from his audience.

The two important things to remember, if notes are being used, is that the eyes should drop to them only for an instant and that when the speaker cuts eye contact with the audience he must maintain voice contact, for if both links are broken he has destroyed whatever spell he has woven. Skilled speakers usually glance at notes to check the next item while finishing their remarks on the present one, and then atone for this brief severance of eye contact by pausing for a calculated visual sweep of the audience.

Reading of speeches, it will be gathered, is absolutely out, and entails certain defeat in any competition. And it's no good pointing to public figures who read their speeches. Often they don't know any better, as may be guessed from their saying "Thank you" at the end. If a speech is a policy statement, or one needing approval in advance or likely to be quoted afterwards, it should be considered as an announcement or a form of communication not dependent on audience reaction.

A speaker must have *command of language* in order to communicate effectively. Though sensitivity to the type of audience is desirable (a strongly intellectual approach not being suited, for example, to a non-intellectual audience), he should use good conversational English and develop a vocabulary, if not already possessing it, which allows him to achieve precision and flexibility of speech. This helps to give him a useful air of authority. Colloquial language needs to be matched to the audience, and provides warmth and humanity so long as it isn't overdone. After all, one who speaks the tongue that Shakespeare spoke should show some appreciation of its rich potential.

Good deportment doesn't mean standing rigidly to attention, any more than effective gesture means emphasising every statement by a wild waving of hands or throwing about of arms.

Pleasing deportment and *gesture* amount very much to doing what comes naturally, so that nobody particularly notices what's being done. If a speaker stands comfortably upright, transferring his weight at times from one foot to another, and doesn't slouch, lean forward, put a hand in his pocket, fiddle with his tie, or do other trivial things which people notice instead of concentrating on what he's saying, his deportment is pleasing. So is his use of gesture if it's restrained, doesn't seem artificial, and bears an identifiable relationship to whatever statement is being emphasised. But, for what it's worth, most Australians depend far less on gesture to assist them in making points than do people of many other countries.

Personality is unquestionably the star part of manner. A persuasive speech isn't just a happy concoction of words but the shape of a speaker's successful presentation of himself to his audience. Personality is built around distinctive individual character and the ability to project it, so that a speaker is recognisable as uniquely himself. It persuades people to accept what he's saying because he's the person saying it. It's a happy combination of eye contact, warmth, sincerity, and such use of voice as is pleasing and effective. Though capable sometimes of being employed to conceal poverty of matter, it's a quality peculiarly fitted to convey a sense of occasion.

"If you elocute, you can't communicate"

It's pleasing to record that elocution, with its affectation and suggestions of insincerity, has now disappeared from the modern public-speaking scene, along with learning speeches by heart and then reciting them, and it's to be hoped that adjudicators working in comparative isolation know this. Nothing gets in the way of a message so strongly as diction which reeks of artificiality. It gives the impression that the speaker's concern is simply to display a hackneyed junior social accomplishment, like playing the piano for visitors, and that the audience's function is no more than to be present in order to applaud. The essential purpose of speaking in public, which is to communicate to people and thereby involve them in what's being said, is lost sight of.

But it should be pointed out, for the the benefit of those persons whom cultural deprivation may have prompted to think the Australian drawl is all, that there's nothing remotely artificial about language spoken with proper regard for its beauty and power.

Opportunities

Once you know what's involved in public speaking, you should put your knowledge into practice. That's no problem if you're already in the habit of making speeches. All you have to do then is to set about achieving greater impact on your audiences so that organisers of meetings will compete with one another for the honour of having you come along to speak.

If you're not in demand, you'll have to make your own opportunities. You can offer to give a talk to a club, society, senior citizens' body, youth group, or any other group, on any subject about which you know something and on which you believe you can speak interestingly. If you're desperate, you can offer to address the local Australian Rules Football or Rugby League club on the virtues of soccer, or vice versa. But, whatever opening you find, you should take a friend with you who understands what you're supposed to do and will criticise your performance soundly. In that way you're likely to learn much faster than if you're merely given so many pats on the back.

If you're within range of an Eisteddfod which includes a public speaking division (such as the City of Sydney Eisteddfod, which accepts entries from all States), or if you're a school student, opportunity awaits you. In the former you may expect to find prepared and impromptu sections, both open and with various age limits to suit school students. Local and regional competitions for the latter are not uncommon, sometimes with regional winners going on to a State final, and State champions progressing to an Australian final. This is the system followed by the Australia-wide schools' public speaking competition for the Plain English Speaking Award, sponsored jointly by the Australian-Britain Society and the Apex clubs and conducted by the Department of Education in each State.

If you're a non-debater entering any kind of public speaking competition you're bound to find considerable difficulty in finishing ahead of, or even alongside, entrants with debating experience of good standard. Of the half dozen or so entrants who win through to a public speaking final (if there were only two finalists it wouldn't really amount to an occasion), most are successful debaters. The point is that debating provides almost unrivalled experience in organising ideas, presenting them methodically, and using personality to capture and hold audience attention. If you wish to attain competitive heights in public speaking you should certainly gain debating experience. And if you're not concerned about the heights, that experience will still help you to gain greater satisfaction from your public speaking than would otherwise be possible.

Beware of inferior models

Now that television has introduced us to the doubtful delight of having all sorts of people addressing us in the living-room, with the danger that we may unwittingly copy inferior models, the warning should be given that not everyone who speaks in public, or speaks to the public in private, can be seriously classed as a public speaker. Certainly there are fewer aggressively uneducated voices to assault our ears than was the case not so many years ago, but we're still asked to endure speeches by public figures who barely move their lips, speak in a dreary monotone, and think the only way to make sure of getting attention is to talk loudly. When they depend on their voices to express views which presumably they consider worth expressing, it's difficult to understand why so few take the trouble to discover how to use their voices either correctly or effectively.

Perhaps the most annoying fault of many politicians and union leaders who are interviewed on television is their projection of the wrong sort of personality, the sort which infuriates anyone who appreciates the power of personality in investing a speaker with credibility. Maybe it's the only sort the fellows have. Few politicians show any sign of pleasant naturalness, warmth, or humour, and many, especially when in opposition, adopt the manner of sneering snarlers. They'd be eliminated, on manner, in the first round of a junior public speaking competition. The same frequently applies to union spokesmen who, by being abrasive, alienate that majority of viewers one imagines they should be seeking to enlist to their causes.

CHAPTER THREE

How To Use Your Voice

When you use your voice you're trying to communicate with people. If you don't know how to use it, "trying" may be all you're doing. People, even when you have them in the captive situation of an audience, don't have to listen to you. But you can persuade them to listen, make them want to listen, if you know how to go about it.

Knowing how to use the voice effectively is necessary, not only for public speakers and debaters, but for everyone who wants to communicate in any kind of situation. And it isn't something which comes naturally, at least not in a complete sense. Its essentials need to be known and consciously put to use.

Aiming for vocal effectiveness

This is a speaker's chief concern, and every aspect of speaking should be viewed in its light. He must use his voice to capture and hold attention. He may stand erect, wear an air of authority, fix his eyes firmly on the audience, make telling use of gesture, have important things to say, and have a sound grasp of his material, but if he can't use his voice effectively all these advantages are cancelled, and he may as well leave the platform without opening his mouth.

Effective use of speech is the ability not merely to talk to people but to communicate thoughts and feelings to them. Communication necessarily includes getting through to them, making them understand and appreciate these thoughts and feelings. And this comes in the first instance through the manner in which the voice is employed.

Vocal effectiveness depends on a combination of these factors: production of speech sounds, voice projection, clarity, vocal quality and use of language.

Production of speech sounds

This depends on *posture* and *breathing*. Although, as speech begins on an exhalation, it's the breath which carries the voice, it's posture which determines how satisfactorily this can be done. The diaphragm and connected muscles support the breath, but only through correct posture, which, in the words of a Quaker saying, is "Head up, also chin; chest out, stomach in". It requires the speaker to stand on the balls of his feet and distribute his weight almost evenly. A slouch, with a sagging middle and flabby waistline, doesn't only prevent the assumption of a desirable air of authority but creates tension in body and neck and robs the voice of much of its necessary breath support. Wrong posture also hinders physical relaxation, without which correct breathing is impossible.

The breath should be taken down by the diaphragm to the deepest part of the chest, so that with its release into sound the whole chest cavity through its vibrations and resonance contributes to the sound, giving it firmness and solidity. The sound becomes uniquely part of the speaker. When sound is made by full use of the breath, less breath is required to make it carry, and speaking becomes easier. If breathing fails to reach the depths of the chest and is therefore shallow, the voice begins in the upper part of the chest, lacks resonance, unpleasantly seems to be pitched higher than it really is, and carries poorly.

It's not proposed to describe the physiological processes by which particular sounds are produced, as this information is readily available. Reference will be made later to faulty production of certain sounds and how to overcome this.

Voice projection

The voice has to be projected in speaking to an audience (words which are allowed merely to fall from the lips only fall to the floor), and the degree of projection required increases with the depth of the hall unless this has been designed, as in the case of a modern concert hall, to achieve something approaching acoustic perfection. There's no question of shouting to be heard (the disadvantages of this will be covered later), or of using a microphone unless the hall is very large indeed.

Projection is achieved by maintaining correct posture and depending more heavily on the diaphragm and associated muscles, not forcing the voice but tucking in the stomach more firmly and so finding greater breath support. It's assisted by precise articulation and greater use of pause.

Projection should be practised. A few sentences, preferably a piece of text demanding variety of pitch, may be thrown at three different objects (or persons) in an audience situation, one close, one in the middle distance, one far away. The breath support should be increased without raising the voice unless it's necessary to do so to be heard comfortably at the extreme range. There should be a mental reaching-out to the object, as this helps surprisingly in reaching it with the voice. Time must also be allowed for sound to reach the object, and that means time for the vowels to carry there and the consonants to make an impact. If the hall has poor acoustics, often an unfortunate result of bare walls and high ceilings, practice is needed in aiming the voice at the floor without dropping the head, in order to reflect it at the audience, and in putting greater force into the consonants.

There are areas where the voice, no matter how well projected, can't be expected to make itself fully comprehensible. One is a dead spot, sometimes found near the centre of a large hall, and the other the distant parts of a very large hall. Wall amplifiers will solve the first problem, but that means using a microphone (normally not recommended in other than the largest halls), and it can be more easily, if somewhat unusually, dealt with by charting the spot boundaries and placing no seats inside them. The second problem can only be solved with microphone assistance.

Microphone technique may be mentioned here. It's necessary to know whether the "mike" is omni-directional. If it is, the speaker doesn't have to speak directly into it. If it isn't, he does, or his voice will fade as he turns his head. It picks up tonal variations with delicacy, but over-emphasises consonant sounds if these are produced with the force which would be necessary if it were not being used. It quickly destroys the speaker's rapport with his audience if he neglects to reduce his volume for the occasion. It hisses at sibilants uttered too close to it, and crackles at anyone who presumes to touch it. If grasped, it reduces the speaker to the abysmal status of a pop vocalist. It should be kept at a steady distance of about fifteen centimetres, ignored as much as possible, and allowed to perform the service for which it's intended.

The chief disadvantage of using a microphone in any but a studio situation is that, like a lectern, it's an artificial barrier between speaker and audience. The speaker is obliged to speak in relation to it and not be conscious only of communicating with the audience. It hinders eye contact. If he uses it regularly he may become careless about voice projection and so lose much of his appeal when he comes to speak without it.

Clarity

Clarity is essential. It doesn't matter how well the voice is produced or projected if the sound can't be understood. When this happens, people stop listening, for, as they see it, if the speaker really wanted them to listen he'd take the trouble to say his words clearly.

Clarity requires that the speaker be audible and intelligible. Audience understanding depends on his ability to convey the exact meaning he intends. To do this he needs to articulate with some precision and to use the various elements of stress. The latter, covered in the next section, are variations in pace, pitch, tone and volume, and use of pause.

Articulation is speaking distinctly, uttering each syllable of a word precisely except where this would create an air of artificiality. A line has to be drawn between carelessness and pedantry. To say "cuppa tea" is careless, "cup of tea" (with "of" fully sounded) pedantic, but "cup 'v tea" (using the indeterminate vowel sound for "o" in "of") natural and acceptable. The points to remember are that vowels (indeterminates excepted) should be clear and reasonably open, consonants firm and clear, and that sounds should be neither run together nor unduly kept apart.

Though changes in vowel sounds are made by altering the shape of the inside of the mouth, the sounds will be blurred and distorted if the lips are not sufficiently shaped to accommodate the alterations. The jaw should be kept loose and flexible, the lips rounded, and the mouth well open to allow the sound to get away freely and to be heard in doing so. Lip-lazy speakers, who are sometimes unexpectedly encountered in high places, lose the battle for clarity so quickly that people rarely try to follow them past the first few woolly sentences.

Consonant sounds need time to make an impact. This applies particularly in a large hall (as mentioned earlier) where, despite proper projection, some degree of volume is required. The further the voice has to carry, the more time must be provided for them. The louder the voice has to be, the crisper the consonants must be to divide the vowels and make up the syllables intelligibly.

Much faulty articulation is a matter of poorly-produced consonant sounds, especially plosives and fricatives.

Plosives are sounds produced by a momentary but complete stopping of the air stream in the vocal tract, followed by a build-up of pressure which is suddenly released. They may be voiced (b,d,g,ch) or unvoiced (p,t,k,j). The articulation error with plosives lies in not stopping the air stream completely, so that "Siberia" almost becomes "Siveria", "plodding" sounds like "plotting", and "beggar" changes to "becker".

The error can be corrected simply by stopping the air stream completely instead of partially, and releasing it positively instead of half-heartedly. A particular advantage in holding on to consonants before letting out the sound is that muscular vibrations are set up, so that the exploding sound contains resonance additional to that produced by making full use of the diaphragm.

Fricatives are produced by narrowing the vocal passage and thereby setting the air stream in vibration by forcing it through a restricted opening. They're also known as continuant consonants because their sounds can continue to be made until the air supply gives out. They may be voiced (v, z, th as in "then", zh) or unvoiced (f, s, th as in "thin", sh). All of them depend for carrying power on the amount of friction allowed to come out. With too much pressure they become like plosive consonants but their sound fails to carry. With too little pressure there's a loss of clarity.

Articulation calls for special attention at the end of a word, especially in passing from a final consonant to an opening one, and more so when the two consonants are the same. "Guinea Go marigo" can't be recognised as the flower variety Guinea Gold marigold, and nobody would take "haw war" for "hall wall". With "what time" the two t's shouldn't be carelessly run together, or completely separated, but should be permitted a slight overlap.

Poor articulation is especially to be deplored because it's nearly always due either to carelessness or to lack of pride in good speech. The form and standards of speech common to persons who articulate badly are often those of others with whom they associate, or of characters in popular television programmes of American origin, particularly the linguistically retarded characters of so many crime and western films.

Exercises in articulation appear at the end of this chapter.

Vocal quality

This is necessary if people are to gain satisfaction or enjoyment from listening to a speaker. It's the imaginative addition to the mechanics of speaking, to voice production and projection, and to clarity. It adds audience appeal to the thoughts being conveyed. It elevates communication to an art and has the power to clothe the framework of speech with a lustrous garment.

Vocal quality begins with the voice itself. Its richness or tonal quality is determined by resonance, which is a reverberation of the air, an amplification of sound, just before it leaves the windpipe, and which uses the upper parts of the vocal system, but also uses the chest as a sounding board. With the nasal sounds (m, n, ng) resonance is produced by diverting the air stream, which carries the voice, through the nasal passages. But it must be remembered that resonance, though occurring just before the sound leaves the body, is dependent on breathing from the deepest part of the chest, and that shallow breathing therefore lacks resonance.

Vocal quality depends next on *how the voice is used*. This concerns the following:
- pace, pitch, tone, volume;
- variations in the use of these;
- pause;
- phrasing, fluency, and rhythm.

The normal *pace* of a speech depends on the type of English, the intention of the words, and the characteristics of the speaker. Interest shouldn't be dissipated by a shortage of words over a given period or by the difficulty of coping with words fired out with great rapidity.

The most pleasing *pitch* for any voice is usually the lowest which can be comfortably accommodated. The higher notes tend to be thin, shrill, and colourless, and will create vocal strain if used too frequently, while the lower ones possess richness and sonority and, when used with full resonance and proper breath support, carry well. It's essential that nervousness be overcome, for that raises the pitch to an unpleasant and harmful degree.

Tone is the voice quality which expresses feeling. It offers a means of saying something and commenting on it at the same time. It reveals the speaker's personal characteristics and often indicates the kind of response he seeks from the audience.

Volume, or loudness, is largely a negative quality. People resent being shouted at, and form the impression that someone who speaks loudly isn't only uncouth but is trying to force his opinions on them. Volume need simply be sufficient, when coupled with projection, to allow listeners in the back rows to hear comfortably.

But it's *variety* which is the spice of speaking. Lack of it produces monotony, which inhibits growth of audience interest and helps to kill any which was there to begin with. Its presence keeps the audience attuned and ensures a favourable reception for many statements which might otherwise attract little attention. Pace, pitch, tone, and volume all offer much scope for variation, while an important associate of change of pace is the pause. All may be used to supply emphasis.

Variation in pace is achieved, not by saying some parts of a speech slowly and then some parts quickly, but by hurrying over relatively unimportant words and taking time over more important ones. Because almost every sentence contains this combination of important and throw-away words, change of pace is built into it. A collection of sentences should therefore feature continuous variation in pace, with the possibility of further modifications through changes in the rate of speeding up or slowing down.

In the sentence "Part of your training as a speaker is to learn to see things from the point of view of the audience", most of the short words are throw-aways. If the words to be speeded up are hyphenated together, the pace pattern appears like this: "Part-of-your training as-a-speaker is-to learn-to see things from-the point-of-view of-the-audience". Because "training" and "point of view" express key ideas they require to be drawn out slightly.

In the sentence "If you can't hear me I'll have to make a better job of projecting my voice", "can't hear me" needs slight lengthening in view of its importance, "I'll-have-to-make-a" runs together, "better job" is lengthened as the second important part, "of" is thrown away, and "projecting my voice" is drawn out most of all because it's the conclusion to which the sentence is really leading.

"If we want to do it, no one is going to stop us" isn't the all-fast sentence those short words seem to indicate, for "no one" needs slight lengthening to achieve emphasis, and "going to stop" should be stretched beyond "want to do" because the conclusion must make greater impact than a condition leading to it.

Minute but necessary changes of pace come into "The only alternative to private competition is government monopoly". "The" and "to" are throw-aways, "is" is half that, and "only alternative" needs more time for the sake of emphasis than does "private competition". "Government monopoly" calls for greater deliberation as the second half of an antithesis.

Variation in pitch should occur continually throughout a speech, creating a profile of undulations. If a straight line represents a flat delivery, an acceptable delivery is shown by a line which rises and falls, with peaks and troughs of different heights and depths, sometimes changing during a word, and often maintaining a higher or lower level for a brief succession of words. A higher level indicates emphasis or feeling, while a dip shows minor words spoken more quickly. The degree of rise or fall varies to suit the shade of meaning to be conveyed, and inflexions (changes of pitch within a word) can be particularly effective.

Pitch variation, perhaps more than anything else, is guaranteed to torture listeners when there's none of it. Continuous assailment by a flat voice turns wakeful people into weary ones, and makes weary ones long for sleep. Should the flat-voice speaker be prompted by the growing frequency of audience yawns to try to command attention by increasing his volume, he makes his deficiency more obvious and excites the antagonism of those he has made sleepy who now can't sleep for the shouting. If a speech is to be robbed of worthwhile effect, lack of pitch variation will surely do it.

Tonal variation is an important means of achieving effectiveness and economy of expression, for a speaker's feelings may be gauged from his tone in a way no amount of explanation can match. For example, "Hello" may be said to a telephone caller in such ways as to indicate "I'm so glad you rang", "I don't like being rung", "I'm suspicious of phone callers", or "I'm in a hurry". Changes of tone are particularly effective in presenting the speaker as a distinct and many-sided individual. But it's important that, despite these changes, pleasantness and warmth be maintained. A contemptuous or harshly critical tone should always be avoided, as unpleasantness can make no appeal to other than unpleasant people and is therefore self-defeating.

Variation in volume needs to be used with caution, and not just because it's almost the only variation to occur to inexperienced speakers. Certainly volume should rise and fall slightly to match the relative importance of words and phrases, but the other variation devices are so finely drawn as to be easily swamped by loudness. An upward change of volume is likely to have an adverse effect on listeners in the front rows, whereas a downward change will have a similar effect on those in the back rows.

Pause, a special form of pace variation, is a device which has to be devised. It's not the same as the audience-losing break which comes when a speaker doesn't know what to say next, consults his notes (the so-called "note pause") to find out, or is trying to cover a lack of material. Its object is to focus attention on what has been said or is about to be said, to prepare listeners for a change of idea, to allow them (and himself) a brief interval for fresh commitment, or to allow the speaker to tap his energy sources or to draw energy from the audience. Without pauses, however slight, there's no opportunity for ideas to be fully absorbed or for their worth, and any highlights in their presentation, to be properly appreciated.

A tiny pause before a word draws attention to it because the hearer, momentarily conscious of an absence of sound, listens with greater care to what follows. This is the most effective way of emphasising a word, especially if pitch is raised for it, because audience ears which haven't lost sensitivity through over-exposure to raucous noises are particularly receptive to moments of silence. This tiny pause also serves the function of separating the different ideas in a sentence.

The speaker needs to gauge with some accuracy the length of pauses designed for the audience to absorb what he's saying. It varies with the number and complexity of his ideas. But he should remember that his job is to be speaking rather than not speaking. To hold a long pause successfully is an accomplishment and a tribute to his personality, but the search for effect must never become obvious.

Phrasing, the breaking-up of sentences into groups of words according to sense instead of punctuation, is necessary to audience understanding. It also simplifies the framing of sentences, which are worked out in phrases to be linked together in various ways, and preserves an air of naturalness. It assists the use of pause, for slight breaks are necessary between phrases if they're not to be run together and their whole purpose to be defeated. But it's worth noting that good phrasing depends on good breathing, for, regardless of its length, a phrase must be adequately sustained with breath.

Fluency is the flow not so much of words as of information. Ideas have to be clothed in words and kept flowing in order to engage and hold audience attention. Hesitation or jerkiness, the latter sometimes due to an exaggerated use of pause, interrupts the flow and allows listener interest to flag. If that happens, the speaker loses rapport, finds his confidence falling away, and has to spend time trying to re-establish himself with the audience when he should be presenting fresh ideas.

There are some hurdles to be surmounted before fluency can be achieved. Um's and er's are an indication that thoughts haven't been properly marshalled, seriously undermine a sense of authority, and provoke listeners to keep a tally of them instead of absorbing ideas. Fluffs (mis-saying of words) show lack of concentration. "Firstly", "secondly", and so forth promise old-style dreariness, and may alarm morning listeners who have no wish to miss their elevenses for an "eleventhly". Unintentional repetition, as opposed to the useful deliberate variety, dams the flow. Casting about for an ending may well submerge all that has gone before.

Rhythm, though defined as "measured flow of words and

phrases", should be one of sense rather than speech. The flow must suit the meaning which the speaker wishes to convey, hastening or lingering over words and phrases as required. Clearly it calls for effective use of variations of pace, pitch, tone, and volume, and a feeling for pause. To speak rhythmically is to present an imaginative interpretation of communication.

Use of language

Because words convey thoughts they need to be chosen and employed with care. Your speech should be instantly understood, fit you as a person, suit audience and occasion, be personal and direct, have variety in sentence structure and some freshness of vocabulary, and be free of errors in grammar and pronunciation.

As a live speech is normally a one-performance affair, you must hit the mark with your first shot. You shouldn't risk obscuring your meaning by using unnecessary words, many-syllable ones when simpler ones will do, those which don't accurately represent your ideas, or those which may mean different things to different people. You should size up your listeners to make sure your words will convey to them the particular meaning you intend.

Your credibility is helped if your words are those which come naturally to you and express your own feelings and ideas. If you're not saying something in your own way, which is often true of a public figure repeating the words of his speech writer, listeners can usually sense it, and then you're on the way to losing them.

Language needs to be appropriate to its circumstances. Simple and fairly colloquial words may suit an informal and relaxed occasion, but scarcely a more formal one. However, there's now an agreeable tendency for formality to be less rigid, except on official or ceremonial occasions, and for persons to be encouraged to speak as individuals. It's now the habitually formal speakers who have the job ahead, and, through difficulty in regaining an informal touch, they may fail to carry conviction.

Language should be personal and direct so that you may form a close relationship with your audience, though "you" needs to be balanced by "we" and "us" to maintain it. Listeners should feel you're speaking expressly to them, not that they're simply the ones who happen to be there when the speech is being delivered.

Variety in sentence structure is a useful part of language, spoken no less than written. Short sentences seize attention, but a succession of them is in danger of creating an impression that your education in English has stopped short or that you want to annoy the audience by firing sharp shots at it. Longer sentences suggest a certain gravity or complexity of ideas, but with them a succession places a strain on comprehension. Obviously a mixture of short and long is necessary. Variation in structure also involves making statements, using exclamatory sentences, asking questions which invite particular answers, or joining sentences in different ways. The form of a sentence in relation to others can be used to produce a contrasting pattern which draws attention to the thoughts being expressed.

Freshness of vocabulary is a valuable interest-builder at a time when so many speakers stamp themselves as purveyors of secondhand ideas by resorting to the latest cliches and vogue words. Nobody wants to hear the moronic "at this point of time" and "in this day and age", or gobbledegook like "meaningful dialogue" and "scenario". Listeners are not impressed by speakers who "commence" when they should "begin", and "utilise" when they should "use", who talk of "in the present circumstances" when they mean "now", or "in the eventuality that" when they mean "if". There are fresh ways of saying things, and audiences, having had so many stale words tossed at them in apparent contempt, are quick to appreciate them.

Vocabulary has other aspects. Matters which are abstract or somewhat complicated are better presented in concrete terms. Inflation, for example, comes to life in terms not of billions of dollars but of the price of a loaf of bread. Sensory images should be used wherever possible, for people are more readily concerned with things if they have the feeling of seeing them, touching them, and so on. Figures of speech (similes, metaphors, hyperbole) are effective when well chosen. Alliteration, despite unending use, rarely fails to make an impact. Intentional repetition of words still pounds an idea home. And nothing beats a strong conclusion, the climax which comes after a review of the major points of the speech.

It shouldn't be necessary to warn speakers to watch their grammar and pronunciation, but it is. Errors in these are not merely those of the uneducated, but of careless persons irrespective of their education. It's time a close season was declared on such crudities as "between you and I", "like I said", "if anyone . . . they", and "these kind of things". Listeners with a reasonable knowledge of English will wince at such childish mistakes, and at mispronunciations such as those listed below. The wincing listeners are the very ones whose acceptance would provide encouragement.

Common pronunciation errors

These are too great a burden for a speaker to carry if he wishes his speeches to be memorable instead of forgettable. Whether they're due to ignorance or carelessness, they incline listeners whose approval is worth having to believe that his ideas are probably as sloppy as his pronunciation. If they're good ideas he ought to be more careful of the company he allows them to keep.

The following list of mispronunciations gives some idea of what speakers should avoid. They're divided into careless errors (elisions, substitutions, intrusions) and those which are largely the result of American influence. Australian English differs in many ways from American English, and educated Australian speakers should take pride in preserving the differences.

Elisions (omission of sounds): ax (acts), arbitry, Artic, Febuary, dimon (diamond), diptheria, guvment, honory, jool, lenth, libary, monop'ly, munce (months), partic'ly, pitcher (picture), pleece (police), proba'ly, reconise, Saddy (Saturday), sec'e'try, temporily, twelth.

Substitutions (replacement of one sound by another): arst (asked), jew (due), git (get), Kosciosko, longjeray ("lanzhree") nealy, piller (pillow), reely, samwidge, Choosdy.

Intrusions (addition of extra sounds): anythink, athaletic, burgular, date'th, drawring, fillum, haitch, heighth, knowen (known), mischeevious, single (signal), umberella.

Errors largely the result of American influence: ad-ult, adversary, advertise-ment, centri-fugal, contrairy, formiddable, harassment, hos-tle (hostile), inte-resting, kilommeter, lab-ora-tory, lootenant, primairily, vaycation, zee (zed).

Critical listening to your own voice

A speaker anxious to improve voice and diction should take every opportunity of listening critically to his speech. To some extent this may be done by speaking with hands cupped over the ears, but the most effective method is to use a tape recorder. During playback he should ask himself certain questions, note the answers he gives, and re-record on a second tape until satisfied he has made the desired improvements. At that stage he may like to erase the first tape, begin listening critically to the second tape, and proceed as before.

These questions, in terms of information supplied in this chapter, are recommended:

● Is normal pace right, and is pace variation well handled?

- Is normal pitch agreeably low, and is pitch variation adequate?
- Is tone pleasant, and is tonal variation used to good effect?
- Is pause used with imagination?
- Is clarity, especially precise articulation, achieved?
- Are phrasing, fluency, and rhythm satisfactory?
- Is the manner of speaking appropriate to the occasion assumed?
- Does the voice reflect the speaker's individuality?
- Are there errors of grammar and pronunciation?

The tape needs to be played many times, as sufficient attention can't be given to more than two questions at the one time. But the time and effort will certainly be repaid, even though influenced by the speaker's ability to recognise his weaknesses and effect the necessary improvements.

Exercises in articulation

These are recommended when listening to tapes indicates there's a need for them. The exercises cover consonant sounds, vowel sounds, sentences of short words (where separation is required), and polysyllabic words (where each syllable has to be given its proper value). They should be recorded and replayed.

Consonant sounds:

The bit of butter Betty bought was bitter.
Peter Piper picked a peck of pickled peppers.
Dauntless daredevils dangled dangerously.
Attempt to tackle a tercel, and talons may tear your tendons.
Gaunt and gawky, Gordon gathered garnets, not galena.
Kebabs, kedgeree, and kippers are kept at this kiosk.
"This cheddar", she chortled, "would get the chop at my shop".
George jogged gingerly past the jeweller's Jaguar.
Vivacity and verve are valuable for vocal variety.
Feathers fall freely from fluttering festoons.
Zebras in zoos think zithers and zodiacs are zany.
Silly Sally sang, simpered, and soon subsided.
Take either this or that, but neither these nor those.
Thirsty and thwarted, we thumped and thundered.
With leisure and treasure, you can measure your pleasure.
She saw seashells on the shelving shore.
Many prime ministers mean much money-making.
Nine nice nuts in a neat green net.
Sing this song when you've sung again the song you just sang.
Be likable and lovable, or you'll be leavable and lonely.
Rioters resolutely refuse to respond to requests.

Haste you, Edward, hat in hand, to the Albert Hall.
Wily women win wealth and wed well.
What did you see, when, where, and why?
Yobbos yawn and yawp, but yokels yowl.
Stop at the top sock shop for socks.
The Leith police dismisseth us.

Vowel sounds:

Hat, ram; face, late; air, where; far, lark; best, lend; see, team; term, heard; pin, rig; ice, night; hot, gone; go, sown; or, ought; oil, coin; house, loud; cup, won; full, book; rule, shoot; use, suit.

Sentences of short words:

If we want to do it, no-one will be able to stop us.

If you need to post that letter, you must first buy a stamp.

He has a big car for sale, and I must talk to him about it.

Polysyllabic words:

Administrative, dependability, individualistic, libertarian, hereditary, regenerative, exuberant, misappropriated, veterinary, valetudinarian.

CHAPTER FOUR

Background To Debating

Competitive and parliamentary debating

Debates are of two broad types, competitive and parliamentary. A debate of competitive type is an argument between two teams of three persons each, or two individuals, or two pairs of individuals, on a particular subject, with the object of establishing the superiority of one view over another. A parliamentary-type debate, which is the parent of the types just mentioned, follows parliamentary practice in being an argument between two groups of persons on a particular motion, with opening and concluding speeches by two opposing leaders. The winner of a competitive debate is decided by an adjudicator appointed for the purpose, whereas the winner of a parliamentary debate is decided by a vote of "the House", composed of all persons present and eligible to take part in it. The essence of both types of debate is not merely the stating of two different viewpoints, but active conflict of argument.

A competitive debate is controlled by a chairman, assisted by a timekeeper, though the chairman may discharge both duties. A parliamentary debate is controlled by "the Speaker". The terms "Mr Chairman" and "Mr Speaker" have been traditionally used in addressing them, though it is now common for "Mr" to be replaced by "Madam" as required. In a competitive debate members of the audience sit where they please, while in a parliamentary debate, where the audience forms "the House" and anyone may speak once he gets the Speaker's call, the usual practice is for supporters of the motion to sit to the Speaker's right, opponents to his left, and for uncommitted members to occupy the rear centre or "cross benches".

The two sides in a competitive debate are known as the Affirmative and Negative, but in a parliamentary debate as the Government and Opposition. By tradition Affirmative debaters and the Government leader, with one or two lieutenants if desired, sit on the chairman's or Mr Speaker's right, while Negative debaters and Opposition leader and his lieutenants sit on the left. Speeches from the front are given from slightly right or left of centre as the case may be.

The motion of a parliamentary debate is set in advance in order to allow adequate preparation. The subject, or topic, of a competitive debate may be known for days or weeks before, or be revealed to the two teams, or be chosen by them, when they assemble for preparation. The sides for a competitive debate are usually announced with the subject when that is set in advance, but with a set preparation time the custom is to toss for sides, and the side winning the toss is required to take the Affirmative.

Team debating

When the teams have to choose one of three subjects, these should be written on a sheet for each team, and the two captains then number them in order of preference. Each team's third choice is eliminated. If two subjects are struck out in this way, the remaining one is the automatic selection. If the third choice is the same for both teams but the first choice is different, they toss to decide which of the other two to use.

In a team debate there are six speakers, three to a team, who speak in Affirmative and Negative order in turn. In certain New South Wales school competitions a team may have a fourth member, known as a co-ordinator or adviser, who assists in preparation before and during the debate but may not deliver a speech except in the rare instance of his being required to replace a colleague suddenly taken ill. Teams which debate additionally outside such competitions are recommended not to use a fourth member even where this is allowed, as it disrupts the training routine for other competitions.

The term "six-speech debate" is sometimes used to distinguish the normal from the reply type, in which there are eight speeches, the seventh being a reply speech by first Negative (two Negative speeches succeeding each other), and the eighth a reply speech by first Affirmative. The reply type is currently used in New Zealand and inter-university debating and some private school competitions. An adaptation of the parliamentary type to competition purposes, it enjoys limited favour in Australia. One disadvantage of it is that it doesn't provide equal opportunity for all speakers unless the practice, unusual in competition circles, is adopted of progressively changing speakers' positions in the team. A second disadvantage is that no clear distinction has been drawn between the functions of the last two speeches on each side. Another is that the roles of third Affirmative and third Negative in reply debating (in which, for example, third Negative may introduce new material barred to him when there is no reply) inevitably differ from those they would have in ordinary debating.

The standard Australian speaking time is ten minutes for each debater. This length applies to adult speeches generally and to those by senior high school students. Year 11 may be regarded as the stage at which any debater with even moderate training can speak for ten minutes. Once he has acquired a certain professionalism he will find it difficult to perform his allotted task in any shorter time. A-grade and interstate adult debaters are often allowed twelve or fifteen minutes, but it has been noted that some are then beset by looseness of structure. Sydney's Year 10 high school competitions allow only eight minutes. The shortest speaking time for any New South Wales competition of note is seven minutes in the City of Sydney under-15 championship. Year 7 debaters, newly introduced to high school debating, begin with four minutes, while upper primary pupils cut their teeth on three-minute speeches. Whatever the length of speech, a warning bell is rung at seventy-five to eighty per cent of the time allowed, with two bells at full time. One authority, perhaps fearing that some speaker may stage a filibuster, requires the bell to be rung continuously when the speaking time is exceeded by one minute.

Parliamentary debating

This closely follows parliamentary practice, sometimes to the extent of having Mr Speaker in a wig and the chief protagonists at a front bench. The motion is proposed by the Premier and opposed by the Leader of the Opposition, and the last two speeches are their replies, given in reverse order. If the debate is to occupy a whole evening, as on a university Union Night, it's usual to select two supporting speakers on each side to be given cabinet or shadow cabinet positions. After opening speeches by the leaders and their lieutenants, the debate is thrown open to "members of the House" to speak alternately for Government or Opposition as they get Mr Speaker's call. On special occasions, such as when invited speakers are present, it is common for prior arrangements to be made to get the call. Interjections, but not interruptions, are allowed. At question time questions may be directed to anyone who has spoken, but only in relation to a matter mentioned by him. The two leaders may not ask questions, and nobody, except these leaders in their reply speeches, may speak to the motion more than once. Mr Speaker is the only person who may be addressed. A member of the House is "the honourable member for (surname)".

Speaking times are arranged to suit the total time available. If the Premier and Leader of the Opposition are given fifteen minutes each for their opening speeches, about half that would be reasonable for their replies. Their lieutenants would then receive ten minutes each, and all other members perhaps five minutes each. The House may grant any speaker an extension of time. In a school situation all times would probably have to be tailored to suit a single or double period.

Parliamentary debating particularly lends itself to lively exchanges of opinion on matters of topical interest. Debates on contentious issues arouse marked interest among members and the general public alike, and many persons may seek a chance to speak. The greater total time than is possible with a team debate permits extended coverage of the field of argument and, because speakers are not limited to six in number, a wider expression of opinion may be expected. A greater range of personalities is revealed, and this brings a heightened sense of realism.

The great advantage of this type of debating to a society or school group, apart from maintaining familiarity with standard meeting procedure, is the opening provided for many members to speak on each occasion instead of waiting to take part in a team debate. As nobody can tell what points will be brought forward, speakers must be alert to follow the flow of argument. This is useful practice for dealing with the sudden changes of approach known in competitive debating. Skill is tested in framing questions, answering them, and dealing with interjections which are often designed to throw a speaker off balance.

Oregon debating

This type, rare in Australia, follows the reply format but adds a cross-examination of each speaker by his successor (for which three minutes are allowed), except that third Negative is questioned by first Affirmative. The reply speeches are exempt from this. The adjudicator gives one mark to the successful examiner or examinee in each encounter and may award a maximum of ten cross-examination marks for any speaker. This type of debating provides a longer and more lively spectacle, and speakers must clearly understand both the logic and content of their cases if they are to emerge unscathed.

Singles

In singles debating there is only one speaker on each side, but each speaks twice. The order is Affirmative opening, Negative opening, Affirmative reply, Negative reply, and the standard times are five, ten, ten, five minutes in turn. Times may be reduced to 4-8-8-4, 4-6-6-4, or 3-5-5-3 with juniors. The Affirmative speaker fills the role of first Affirmative in his opening speech, and of both second and third in his reply. The Negative speaker does the work of first and second Negative in his opening, and of third in his reply. The double time is for a double duty in each case.

Singles is an important activity. It teaches self-reliance, for a singles debater has no colleague to attempt retrieval of the case if he has failed to secure it. It teaches him to think quickly, for success in this form of debating often depends on ability to seize the initiative at very short notice. It shows him the need for flexibility of approach, for he must suit the needs of the situation instead of following a pattern established for him in the team. It gives him one-debate experience of two other roles beside the one he normally plays, and is useful to him in representative teams where he will often be required to take an otherwise unfamiliar position. Singles in a school arouses much interest through its quality of individual combat, instant variety, brevity, and the ease with which it can be adapted for such competition purposes as finding the school's champion debater.

Pairs

Pairs debating, little known despite its undoubted value, has no established format but perhaps best follows that of singles, though with four speakers to carry the four speeches. Under this format, with the range of speaking times as shown for singles, the first Negative and second Affirmative receive double time. Its importance as a training exercise is that it offers an opportunity for a team of three members and a reserve to practise together without having to enlist two inferior speakers to make up two normal teams. It gives the reserve the necessary experience of debating in good company. It provides variety as a preliminary to a major debate.

Instant debating

This has been used with great success as a training and exhibition device. No preparation time whatever is permitted. A speaker, on being called by the chairman, is given a subject and asked to speak for or against it, usually with a time allowance of three or four minutes. In its simplest form, speakers occupy team positions at tables but speak individually on different subjects, each giving a first Affirmative or first Negative speech according to whether he has been placed on the chairman's right or left. Each Negative speaker is required to create an air of authenticity by spending some of his time attacking a case which he imagines he has just heard.

The instant approach may also be used to add diversity to singles, pairs, and team debating, all of which proceed on a similar shortened basis from a beginning as previously indicated. This, which may be termed the initial-instant variety, is only instant debating as far as the first speaker is concerned, but it's very much a matter of instant preparation for all other speakers. Succeeding Affirmative speakers share the Negative's disability in not knowing what the Affirmative case is until they hear it as the opening speaker manufactures it. In no other form of team debate, for instance, will five speakers be found listening so intently to every word spoken by first Affirmative, for they have to discover the Affirmative line, note the break-up of the case, and then prepare to support or attack that case.

Nothing matches the power of instant debating, of whatever variety, in concentrating speakers' minds on the fundamental issues of debating and in forcing them to think quickly and soundly. Equally, nothing matches its power, when displayed by alert and competent speakers, to hold an audience spellbound. The debaters seem to be doing the impossible.

The technique is relatively simple. The subject has to be reasonably straightforward, and the Affirmative must be required to keep it that way. The opening speaker handles definition and subject analysis quickly, asks himself why the proposition is true and thereby establishes a line, justifies a selection of two aspects of his case, and develops and illustrates these. He needs to project his personality vigorously both as normal practice and as a means of overcoming any doubts engendered by the abnormal haste.

Audiences are not normally aware of any simplicity about instant debating. To them it's a new kind of magic. They become fired with fresh enthusiasm for debating, and the debaters among them are quick to draw appropriate conclusions which are likely to lead to marked improvement in their own efforts.

Television debates

These are most successful in parliamentary form, as has been evident from Australian Broadcasting Commission Monday Conference telecasts featuring outstanding senior high school debaters. The method, as practised on these occasions, is for six hand-picked speakers to be divided between the two front benches, prior arrangements to be made for certain others in the audience to get the call, and an opportunity to be provided for further ones who might jump to their feet. Editing to fit a time slot ensures that only the most successful speakers among the audience take part in the screened program, except that the need to present speakers in pairs (one Government, one Opposition) may give screen time to an occasional speaker who doesn't quite deserve it. Use of tiered seats allows the audience to be presented as individuals. Speaking times have to be sharply reduced, but capable debaters, especially when allowed to rise to their feet, can make a strong impression in three or four minutes.

Televised team debates which sometimes appear on commercial stations are deprived of much of their appeal if the debaters are required to speak from a sitting position behind a table. This unnatural attitude cuts off a speaker from the audience which it's his business to persuade, and makes it difficult for him to project his personality. His facial expression is almost the only "manner" open to him. Reading, or excessive dependence on notes, becomes very obvious in close-up. Presentation in this form does nothing for debaters or debating.

What's often termed a debate between two or more public figures who accept an invitation to state their views on some controversial matter for the edification of television audiences is not a debate at all, but merely an expression of widely different opinions. It's a case of "I've come prepared to say this and to take no notice of anything you say, and nothing will prevent me from saying it or will make me take you seriously". The only advantage a debater is likely to derive from it is to note, for avoidance purposes, crudities of manner and an impressive list of common errors of reasoning, both of which tend to increase when a public figure, who would lose prestige if proved wrong, is cornered.

Duties of speakers

These duties in standard (non-reply) team debating, and as adapted to singles and pairs, are outlined here but developed further in Chapter 6. A correct understanding and application of them is necessary for the debate to get off the ground.

First Affirmative has to define necessary words in the subject, analyse it (that is, review possible interpretations of its meaning, settle for one, and explain why), state the theme or "line" which the team intends to follow (usually found by asking why the proposition is true), work up to two (normally no more) basic aspects of its case, allocate one to himself and the other to his second member, develop his own share of the argument, and finish by reviewing what he has said. In a ten-minute speech he will generally begin development after about four minutes.

First Negative is required to agree or disagree with the definition and subject analysis given, explain any disagreement, refute the Affirmative line (with little reference to individual points) in terms of the Negative line, work up to two basic aspects of his team's case, develop his part of the argument, and present a review. Development may be postponed until half way through if the Affirmative approach requires considerable attention. Interwoven in his speech should be a contrast of the two cases to the Negative's advantage. He should avoid making defeat certain by entering on a "definition debate" (that is, disputing the definition but not the case based on it) or setting up an invalid argument (disputing, not the Affirmative case, but merely its right to put that case).

Second Affirmative, before attempting to develop the second strand of his team's case, must re-examine definition if necessary and deal with the Negative case, for if that case retains much of its strength after he has spoken, his team's task will become difficult. He plays a critical role in being the first speaker for the side, with only one colleague to follow, after the Negative has shown its hand. He may reasonably defer development until the mid-point of his speech.

Second Negative should follow second Affirmative's pattern except for extent of refutation, for that should have received adequate attention from his leader. However, he needs to re-inforce that refutation and to deal with second Affirmative's efforts to recover the initiative. If he performs those two tasks quickly and efficiently he may expect to devote two-thirds of his speech to development.

Both third speakers have much, though not quite, the same work to do, but emphatically it's not to spend eight minutes in refutation and the last two minutes in summary. That idea was thrown out when the notion of continual conflict came in. Third Affirmative may argue a further strand of his team's case but is strongly advised against doing so and thereby reducing the time available for refuting second Negative's points and still discharging the general duty described below. Third Negative may not develop his team's case further or introduce any new matter, as nobody remains to answer him.

The basic duty of any third speaker is to contrast the two cases to the advantage of his own. He should deal with general rather than particular aspects of both cases, except that third Affirmative, as stated above, needs to cover specific points made by second Negative. A third speaker has two strong approaches open to him. He may review the opposing case, show why it should be discarded, review his own, show why it should be preferred, go over his opponents' chief arguments with the object of demolishing them, and finish with a summary showing favourable contrast. Or, after setting up the basic contrast to his team's advantage, he may dispose of major arguments in such fashion as to emphasise his team's reply to each of them and so work to an effective conclusion.

The duties of singles speakers may be explained simply. The Affirmative opening corresponds to a first Affirmative speech, the Negative opening to a combined first and second Negative, the Affirmative reply (not well named) to a combined second and third Affirmative, and the Negative reply to a third Negative with the same restriction on new material. The duties of pairs debaters, in following the singles pattern, may be readily inferred.

Chairman's duties

The chairman's first duty is to check basic arrangements, such as seating of teams, adjudicator, and audience, provision of glasses of water for speakers and adjudicator, and presence of bell and stopwatch. (If the two latter are missing, debating isn't being taken seriously enough). When the teams and adjudicator are in position, he should announce the competition (if any), the subject to be debated, names of teams and their members in speaking order, adjudicator's name, times at which a warning bell, and then a final double bell, will be sounded. He is to demonstrate these rings for the benefit of the teams. He should introduce each speaker at the adjudicator's signal. At the end of the debate, when signalled, he invites the adjudicator to give his decision. The chairman's final duty is to call for a vote of thanks from the losing team, then from the winning team, and to close the debate.

Now when even junior school debaters may speak with much verve, the chairman should not draw unkind attention as the unimpressive one of the speakers. While being careful not to upstage the debaters, he should project a pleasant personality in order to put the speakers at ease and give the audience an agreeable sense of occasion.

Marking

Marking of team speeches conforms to a maximum of 40 for matter, 40 for manner, 20 for method. The possible total for a speaker is 100, and for a team 300. In reply debating the present practice seems to be to award a 50 maximum (20,20,10) for each reply speech, giving a team maximum of 350. In singles and pairs debating the maximum is 50 for the short speech, 100 for the long one, and 150 overall.

CHAPTER FIVE

How To Prepare A Debating Case

"Never make it easy for the other side"

This is a maxim which every debater should repeat when starting preparation. Success doesn't usually reward the team which enters the conflict with inferior weapons. A weak case offers an immediate advantage to the opposition. Teams which have acquired much skill in arguing the Negative don't need to have things made easy for them by the Affirmative. The same teams, when Affirmative, are experienced in finding faults in the Negative case on which their second speaker may pounce. Sometimes it's difficult to win with a good case, but, unless the opposition lacks both perception and tactical skills, it's extremely difficult to win with a poor one. That's just as it should be, because it's no function of debating to reward shoddy thinking.

The amount of preparation isn't nearly so important as its quality. An hour spent preparing a case which invites attack is an hour wasted. A half-hour's preparation is probably enough for a competent team, and there are instances of sound cases having been prepared in much less. It's better to be under-prepared but with a solid theme which allows ready off-the-cuff speaking than to be over-prepared even with a sound theme, and to have no hope of covering a multitude of points in sufficient detail to make them count. The idea is to have only a few strands to the argument but to make sure they will bear its weight, to expand and illustrate each one, and to remember that nearly half the total time must be devoted not to exposition of the case but to conflict.

Definition

Preparation begins with definition and subject analysis, and if it doesn't surmount those two hurdles it may as well end there. Definition is required of every word having significance in terms of the subject, and then the meaning of the whole subject, which isn't always just the sum of its words, has to be worked out. After that even the most seemingly simple subject has to be analysed in order to establish its broader meaning, and an interpretation adopted which is reasonable and capable of supporting a useful argument.

Few words have only one meaning. Reference to the Oxford Dictionary (the only one for standard English) makes that clear. The most suitable meaning is the most reasonable one, usually in an Australian context. A word may even mean whatever it can reasonably be shown to mean. As definition is the duty of first Affirmative, the meanings he attaches to words will stand unless the Negative can give sound reasons for rejecting them, and even if the Negative does this it must still dispose of the case built on them. But capable Negatives can do these things.

What, for instance, is meant by "society", "students", "modern music", and "Australia"? Is "society" mono-cultural, multi-cultural, our Australian variety, or upper-class people? Are "students" secondary, tertiary, persons who attend any educational institutions, or all persons studying in any kind of situation? Does "modern music" relate to any contemporary music, only to fine music, or only to music in the popular idiom? And what limits are set to "modern"? Is "Australia" the country, or its people, or both?

Unless good reason exists, definition shouldn't be narrowed to suit a particular case lest the other team secure an advantage by justifiably broadening it. If the definition is broad to begin with, the other team will do well to seek advantage from narrowing it to fit a more acceptable frame of reference.

Seven types of subjects

While the ingenuity of persons who set debate subjects is boundless and every subject should be viewed with suspicion, it happens that subjects fall into a small number of categories, though one subject can often be classified under more than one heading. It's useful to know what's likely to be involved in preparing a case on a certain kind of subject. Subjects may:
● depend on key words or phrases;
● involve some form of comparison;
● turn on "should";
● concern the truth of the proposition;
● require interpretation;
● be light;
● be controversial.

The subject must be examined for key words or phrases, as they point the argument in a precise direction. Before planning a case supporting "That we watch too much television" it's necessary to decide how much is too much and be able to justify that decision.

"That in delay there lies no plenty" hinges on "plenty", which in this context means "considerable advantage". "No longer" is the key to "That the strike is no longer a fair weapon", and this involves comparison, the next type. It should be emphasised that many debate subjects, of whatever type, contain key words and phrases and that a team missing them delivers itself to the opposition.

Comparisons need setting up, with an account of the respective features of the things being compared, before one can be shown to possess more of something than the other. In "That publicity is a better salesman than quality" it isn't a matter of proving that publicity sells things and quality doesn't, but of stating how each sells things and then proving that publicity sells them better, that is, more easily and in greater quantity. The comparison in "That the shorter the better" isn't stated but obviously is with "longer". In "That we need more freedom" it's a question of comparing the amount of freedom we have with the larger amount we're to be shown to need.

"Should", as far as debate subjects go, is often difficult to prove in the context of moral obligation, and is better taken as putting forward a fairly compelling reason for taking a certain course of action. "That we should speak our minds" doesn't suggest we're obliged to do so, any more than "That we should count up to ten" suggests there's a moral reason for every sort of hesitation.

When the *truth of the proposition* is at stake it's necessary to marshal evidence to support it, and the debate should largely be an exercise in logical thinking. There is no limit to subjects of this type, and some which come to mind are "That there is a never-ending audacity of elected persons", "That we wish to be deceived", and the now famous "That life wasn't meant to be easy".

Subjects requiring interpretation are those of which the meaning must first be established. This calls for care if there can be no generally accepted meaning, as in "That the trees are full of galahs" (which has been successfully argued, at interstate adult level, from the viewpoint that the upper echelons of power are filled by persons who make noisy spectacles of themselves) or "That the grapes are sour" (which can be taken as indicating a common habit of pretending we don't want something when we can't get it). On a less esoteric plane are "That time's a-wasting" and "That the contest is enough".

Under this heading come traps for literalists. "That you never can tell" can't be taken literally, for the Negative would only have to produce a single exception to disprove the proposition and commit the unpardonable sin of reducing the debate to childishness. It must be taken as a popular saying expressing the frequency of our uncertainty about people and things. Similarly with "That women are a different species", which is literally untrue and can only be argued in terms of differences in their attitudes and actions.

Light subjects are intended to provide scope for entertainment. "That only mugs work", "That putting things over keeps us in clover", and "That the more the merrier" all lend themselves to witty comment on persons and attitudes, delight audiences, and polish the image of debating. However, before the preparation room can be turned into a joke factory, debaters should remember that humour worth remembering is a product of personality and style, not of cheap gags, and that even the lightest treatment requires to be grounded in a basis of argument lest the gate be left open for the other side.

Controversial subjects are rarely set for school debates, for there's the problem of emotional, and perhaps ideological, involvement. If a controversial subject, such as "That strikers are enemies of the people" or "That zero population growth should be enforced", has to be debated, preparation must centre on facts and adopt a broad perspective. Bias versus bias isn't debating, and bias on one side only can easily be swept aside by resort to evidence. However, if school students were given practice in debating controversial subjects they would probably develop logical and mature attitudes which are lacking in so many of today's adults.

Constructing a case

"That the pen is mightier than the sword", even though hoary with age, gives an idea of what's involved in analysing a subject. The metaphorical terms "pen" and "sword" must be translated into normal language, which isn't as easy as it seems. Does "pen" mean the instrument, including printing, with which ideas are reproduced, and, by extension, the printed material? Does it include the user of the pen, who seeks to influence people through his ideas? What does "sword" mean at a time when swords have almost gone out of use? What is "might", so that we can understand "mightier"? Does the word "is" imply the present, or the past and present but not necessarily the future, or does it imply a permanent state of affairs?

When an interpretation of the subject has been decided, it's time to begin constructing the case. The best method is to ask why the proposition is, or is not, acceptable, and to find a sound answer which can be presented under two worthwhile and distinct aspects to be divided between the first two speakers. This answer becomes the theme around which the case is built and which should give it consistency and strength.

Points for the Affirmative

The Affirmative, in properly seeking to limit the Negative's options, shouldn't create trouble for itself. The self-defeating invalid case will be mentioned later. An off-beat case, devised to surprise the Negative, may succeed brilliantly, but on the other hand may be difficult to sustain if attacked on the ground of unreasonableness. It would be unwise, for example, to argue "That Big Brother is watching you" in terms of over-size brothers watching family members to make sure they don't take up too much room, or to present "That power corrupts" in the context of high-powered cars corrupting the morals of young drivers and their pick-up passengers.

It's advisable for an Affirmative to give some thought, during preparation, to possible Negative replies and how to combat them. "How would we try to refute these points we're making?" If it seems that refutation wouldn't present much of a challenge, the points should be discarded. If that criticism could be made of the whole case, then it should be discarded in favour of a stronger one. But if likely Negative replies can be prepared for, the team gains assurance, which, though this may be reduced should the attack develop differently, will certainly be strengthened if the attack is made along weaker lines.

Where preparation has been considered in this chapter from the Affirmative angle, as has often been the case, this is because a debate develops, or fails to develop, in relation to the pattern set by the Affirmative. Put simply, the Affirmative will normally win if its case isn't successfully refuted, whereas the Negative will normally win if it successfully refutes the Affirmative case, though it must be recognised that reading of speeches or serious under-time may change the situation.

Points for the Negative

All general advice on preparation applies equally to both sides. The Negative team, however, must always keep one extremely important fact in mind. No matter how exquisite a case it prepares, that case has value only in relation to the case put by the Affirmative. Should the latter take an unexpected line, the Negative may have to throw away its prepared case and plan a new one while first Affirmative is speaking.

The requirement that the Negative case must relate to the Affirmative one is well illustrated in the predicament of a Negative team which finds itself having to argue the case it had expected the other would argue. An instance at high-school level concerned the subject "That pop stars should pop off", where the Affirmative, instead of denigrating pop stars, argued that they should perform even more explosively (on the analogy of champagne corks popping) than at present. The only way out of that was for the Negative to denigrate the people it had planned to defend, but this particular Negative wasn't equipped to handle the situation.

One lesson to be learnt from this is that a team shouldn't prepare its case in as much detail when Negative as when Affirmative, for the Negative can't tell how far its case will be relevant until first Affirmative has shown his hand. This applies even more strongly in singles debating, where the Affirmative speaker often seeks a tactical advantage by prolonging subject analysis and withholding his line until fairly late in his opening speech in the hope of forcing the Negative into some change of case with only a minute or so in which to prepare that change. The time saved by the Negative in reduced preparation should be spent in considering possible Affirmative approaches and suitable replies to them.

The Negative, despite not knowing what the Affirmative may come up with, mustn't omit punch from its preparation. The chances that a bright Negative will be taken by surprise are not great, as it should have considered what to do with likely Affirmative cases. Its business is to prepare the positive Negative case it hopes to argue, though modifications may be necessary in the light of what first Affirmative says.

Use of the term "positive Negative" emphasises the kind of approach the Negative should take in its preparation. Gone are the days when it was thought good enough for the Negative to tag along behind the Affirmative, merely expressing an opposite viewpoint after first bewailing having drawn the so-called "wrong side". Now it's usual for a capable team to rejoice at being Negative, for the chances of putting pressure on the other team are often increased thereby. The Negative's job in preparation is first to plan a rebuttal of the expected Affirmative case and then to plan a counter-case which the Affirmative must try to refute. This is a tactical move to make the Affirmative fight on two fronts, for it then has both to defend and develop a case which has been attacked by the Negative and to attack a Negative argument which wasn't revealed until first Affirmative had already committed his team. A team must stay committed or lose, though, if the opposition plays the right cards, it may stay so and still lose.

Four standard Negative approaches

Both teams should be guided in preparation by awareness of the four standard Negative approaches. The Negative will have to adopt one of them or be rightly accused of trying to muddle through. They are:
- straight negation;
- "not generally true";
- proving the converse;
- changing the direction of argument.

Straight negation is not recommended unless there seems no useful alternative, for, as stated above, it exerts no unusual pressure on the Affirmative. Among subjects which don't appear suited to refutation by any other approach, however, are "That religion is out of date", "That society can survive without the family", and "That we should stop smoking". Usually the proposition is an absolute capable of rebuttal only by another absolute. Persons who invite a battle of the absolutes by setting subjects calling for this Negative approach should consider the possibility that a debate will be spoilt by displays of prejudice.

"Not generally true" is a Negative approach with a great deal to recommend it. It allows creation of an air of sweet reasonableness in accepting the truth of the proposition in some circumstances, to be followed by proving that in a majority of instances, or in a significant number of important instances, it is not true. This amounts to showing, to quote from a song in Gershwin's "Porgy and Bess", that "it ain't necessarily so". The Affirmative is placed under pressure to prove the proposition to be more often true than not. Even clearly being in such a position will be damaging if it had unwisely begun by taking an absolute stand. Debaters should always allow themselves room for acceptable manoeuvre.

Proving the converse, not often possible, also puts strong pressure on the Affirmative. It amounts to a reversal of the proposition. With this approach, "That girls are more deceitful than boys" is attacked by arguing that boys are more deceitful than girls. If the necessary comparison is set up and the converse proved, the original statement has been disproved, as both can't be true.

Changing the direction of argument, or using a variation within a negative framework, bears some similarity to the "not generally true" approach. Obviously it's useless to run off at a tangent and fail to make direct contact, but the Affirmative may be placed in difficulty if it can be steered along an unfamiliar path, especially if it had left the gate open. An example is countering "That variety is the spice of life" by taking "the" as the key word and showing variety to be only one of many spices. Another is combating "That intolerance is more dangerous than ignorance" by arguing that both are dangerous but that ignorance is rather more so, perhaps with a proving-the-converse twist to expose intolerance as a product of ignorance.

All arguments require proof

It must be remembered that the Affirmative's duty is to prove its case, and the Negative's duty is to disprove that case and if possible to prove its particular variation of it. Teams would do well to adorn their preparation rooms with the warning, "If you can't prove it, don't say it". They should constantly be reminded that what are variously termed sweeping statements, assertions, assumptions, or generalisations are worth nothing. For every argument advanced during preparation, the evidence should be noted beside it or, if this can't be produced, it should be discarded. The reason, in debating terms, is not so much that a capable adjudicator will notice the error and begin deducting matter marks as that the other team will notice and produce contrary evidence.

Debaters must learn what constitutes proof, and disproof. A single piece of evidence won't make or break an argument. But total proof isn't necessary either, is usually impossible, and if it were possible would render debate impossible. What's required is the production of telling illustrations to make the truth of the argument appear most probable. Alongside the "if you can't prove it" warning should be placed the maxim "Find a significant number of important instances". To take their minds off the labour of writing this up, debaters can share a chuckle over their fellows who, in the fond belief that they're supplying evidence, quote statistics as a result of reading somewhere that "a million Frenchmen can't be wrong" and quote statements by alleged authorities through having been nurtured in an exaggerated respect for persons who happen to be placed over them.

Care should be taken in choosing proof examples. Attempted proof by selected instances is an error of reasoning because it involves only those things which favour a case and ignores the existence of others, often equally obvious, which injure that case. The Affirmative needs to avoid this error and so deny the Negative an easy opening, while the Negative, if seizing the opening, needs to do more than produce a new lot of instances which, though true, don't destroy the truth of the first lot. All sorts of things may be true at the same time. The moral is that a team's examples, to achieve their full value, must be tied to a constant theme, which, to achieve its full value, must be in clear opposition to that of the opposing team. This means that each team, in preparing its case, must keep its theme constantly in mind and closely relate arguments to it.

Invalid Affirmative and Negative

The worst mistake a debating team can make is to indulge in that mind-boggling display of wasted effort, the invalid case. It's not necessarily fatal for a team to have a minor flirtation with an invalid argument, but to construct the whole case invalidly is to head for certain defeat. An invalid case simply cannot win a debate, even if the opposing speakers make only token appearances, have poor presentation, and don't understand the conflict.

An invalid Affirmative case is one which shuts out the Negative, denying it any possibility of entering the argument. To argue "That there are no more statesmen", for example, on the ground that statesmanship has never existed and cannot exist is suicidal. The Affirmative must accept the fact that there can be a case against it and then set out to disprove that case.

An invalid Negative case is one which disputes the Affirmative's right to put its case and therefore makes no attempt to refute that case, or which centres on an unrelated issue to the exclusion of direct conflict, or disputes the Affirmative's definition but not the case built on it. This last, known as a definition debate, is a fault of preparation during instead of before the debate, and will be covered in Chapter 6.

The first invalidity is shown in an attempt to destroy a case for "That democracy is on trial" by arguing that there isn't such a thing as democracy, or a case for "That Jack is as good as his master" by asserting that it's fundamental to the man-master relationship that a man can never be the equal of his master. To quarrel with the subject is a foolish exercise in quarrelling with whoever set it and dodging the matter at issue. "That pop concerts are a culture hazard" can't be refuted by arguing that pop concerts are a development of culture and that culture can't be a hazard to itself. An impossible reply to "That trade unions need a new image" is that they don't need an image and so can't need a new one.

An example of the case that's invalid because it's unrelated is one which sought to dispose of "That we think about our rights when we should be thinking about our responsibilities" by contending that we should be thinking about our wrongs. Another attacked "That racial equality is an impossible ideal" on the ground that equality of opportunity was the impossible ideal. Changing the direction of argument is a sound tactic, but any attempt at changing the whole basis of the argument is self-defeating. To insert new words in the subject means creating a fresh subject, and debating that one can't possibly affect an argument on the original one.

Organisation of restricted preparation

How is this best done? Which member does what in preparation? How far do members prepare separately, and how far together? How is work distribution varied when a reserve or non-speaking fourth member shares in preparation? Where a dispute occurs, is there a way of resolving it so that precious time isn't wasted? These are questions to which teams and their coaches (the latter not being allowed to contact their teams during restricted preparation) should know the answers.

A sound Affirmative time division for an hour's preparation is twenty minutes together, thirty minutes apart, ten minutes together. In the first period decisions need to be reached on definition, interpretation of the subject, the all-important line to be adopted, possible replies by the other team and how to handle them, and allocation of material to the first two speakers. In the second period the plans of the first two speeches are worked out, points sorted into the best order, and examples found to support them. In the final period the team reviews the whole case so that each speaker knows what his partners will be saying and any difficulties may be ironed out. If preparation has to be condensed into a shorter time, corresponding time reductions should be made. The Negative time division may differ to the extent of allowing extra time in the first period for deeper consideration of the other team's possible approaches and a suitable response to them, and for testing the proposed Negative case against likely Affirmative reactions before making a firm commitment to it.

The work of the first two speakers may be gathered from the above. The third speaker, with no development of the case on his own part to occupy him, and as comparison of cases is his major concern, should check out all likely conflict between the two cases and decide how his team's interest may be best served. In the second period he should assist the other speakers and prepare a summary of the argument and select key points for his own review.

Use of fourth members, even when permissible, isn't favoured by professional-type debaters and their coaches. If there is one, such as the reserve to a representative team, who can scarcely be excluded from preparation, he will learn from working with the three speakers in turn and can be given the special task of finding examples and preparing openings, endings, and highlights.

Disputes are best resolved in short order by a team captain, who must enjoy the confidence of both team and coach, and should either be the third speaker or one who is competent to check the latter's preparation performance and advise him and their mutual colleague as may seem necessary. A captain's snap decision may sometimes turn out to be wrong, but there must be no complaining about it unless it's thought necessary to replace him. During the debate his generalship may be of great value.

CHAPTER SIX

How To Present A Debating Case

Presenting a debating case is sometimes thought of as making effective use of matter, manner, and method. Matter is both that prepared before the debate and that prepared during the debate in response to developing situations. Manner is how, in an individual sense, that matter is presented. Method is the structure of a speech, the observance by a speaker of the duties of his position in the team, and the contribution he makes to teamwork. But it's sound practice to think of matter and method in combination as the two elements of conflict, and of manner as the vehicle by which the ideas of conflict are conveyed.

Use of the initiative

Effective debating calls for proper use of the initiative. First Affirmative should try to establish an initial advantage for his side and thereby render the Negative's task difficult. First Negative's aim is to dispose of any such advantage and capture the initiative by placing pressure on the Affirmative. Second Affirmative's job is to overcome this pressure and regain the initiative by re-establishing the favourable position set up by his first speaker. Second Negative then has the task of damaging the re-established Affirmative case sufficiently to put the Negative argument once more in the ascendant. The two third speakers continue the battle of the initiative in their comparison of cases, and victory usually goes to whichever team is in possession of this advantage at the end.

   Not all debates follow this pattern. If first Negative fails to come to terms with the original case, the initiative remains with the Affirmative and can be reinforced by that side's second speaker, giving second Negative an uphill task in trying to retrieve the situation. On the other hand, a skilful first Negative may use one of the standard approaches so effectively as to place the Affirmative in a difficult position or, if there's a basic weakness in its case, drive it into a corner from which there's little chance of escape. Through use of the initiative, or failure to use it, debates are often won by first Negatives, lost by them, or lost by second Affirmatives.

In these days when every well-coached team, as Negative, sees itself with some justification as a giant-killer, Affirmatives need to employ precise technique to offset the advantage possessed by the other side in being able to reply to every one of their speeches. The Affirmative case should be carefully planned, developed, and protected against attack, the Negative case hit hard where it seems most vulnerable, and each speaker should discharge his duties with care and precision. Third Affirmative must make a last strengthening of the defences against the inevitable final assault.

Avoiding a definition debate

Should the Negative find the Affirmative definition unacceptable, it needs to avoid getting into a "definition debate" and thereby organising its own downfall. Such a debate, as mentioned previously (Chapter 5), is an invalid-Negative type in which the definition is disputed but not the case built on it, the Negative then running off at a tangent to argue a case founded on a new definition. If, for example, with "That more bridges should be built", the Affirmative took "bridges" metaphorically as social and cultural links between people, arguing that we should create more of them, and the Negative took "bridges" literally (as, say, steel or concrete objects), arguing, without reference to the Affirmative case, that we have enough of them already, the Negative must lose the debate.

Remembering that an Affirmative case which is allowed to stand, no matter what it is standing on or what its quality, is almost automatically a winning case, the only course open to the Negative is to accept the "unacceptable" definition briefly, purely for the purpose of smartly disposing of the Affirmative case based on it, and then to replace the definition by a more reasonable one, being careful to present solid grounds for doing so. The Negative then constructs and develops its case in terms of the new definition. The Affirmative is thus placed in an awkward facing-two-ways situation, having to attack a case built on what has been shown as a more reasonable definition and to defend and develop its own case built on a definition shown to be less reasonable. An Affirmative should avoid any definition which may expose it to this form of attack, but a Negative team should consider carefully whether the Affirmative definition and consequent case may not possess sufficient strength to survive the attack and leave the Negative in a hole of its own digging. It's not surprising that most

Negatives prefer to make the best of a bad definition and scrap a prepared case in order to confront the Affirmative throughout.

What matters is whether the Negative, which naturally would prefer not to fight on unfamiliar ground, can carry debating's "average reasonable man" with it in its march to a more suitable arena. With "That more bridges should be built" a change from actual bridges to community links can easily be supported, as it's clearly more important to weld society together than to bridge more rivers, and the Affirmative's task in recapturing the initiative is unenviable. If the Affirmative, as once happened, argues "That the fast buck should return to the wilderness" in the context of a sexually excited male deer leaving settled areas and heading for wild country where the opportunities for sexual activity are greater, the Negative wouldn't be at risk in refuting this on the basis that he wouldn't necessarily achieve his object, and then, after showing that a more acceptable definition of "fast buck" relates to making money quickly and unscrupulously, setting out to prove that persons who engage in this are displaying business acumen in seizing opportunities presented to them and don't deserve to be ostracised for it.

The Negative would scarcely have reason on its side if, with "That we are a provincial people", it disposed of an Affirmative case built on "provincial" as "narrow-minded" and then put forward one based on the meaning "living in the provinces", arguing that most Australians live in our major cities and therefore aren't provincial. The Negative would also be at the mercy of its opposition if, with "That dogma is the enemy of truth", it opposed "church doctrine" to "arrogant declaration of opinion", for the case that the latter is hostile to truth is too weighty for quick dismissal.

Special applications of matter and method

This supplements the coverage of matter and method given in Chapter 2.

Good *matter* is always better for reinforcement. The team's line should be emphasised several times in every speech, and all arguments should be tied to it, for the line is always more important than the points, essential as they may be in their own right, which lead up to and illustrate it. Repetition of the line, if it's sound, makes the case clearer and more impressive, and exerts subtle pressure on the team which has to disprove it. Sound advice on the whole treatment of matter is: "Tell them what you're going to tell them; tell them; then finish by telling them what you've told them".

Method in a debating speech is its organisation both internally and as part of a team case. It concerns not only what's planned in advance but what has to be planned as the debate progresses. It's not a vague associate of matter but something closely intertwined with it in the concept of conflict. It mustn't be dismissed as a minor thing worth only twenty per cent of total marks, but be looked on as a major item which combines with matter for sixty per cent of total marks. Even on its own, method is often the deciding factor in a debate between two well-matched teams.

A speech should be constructed according to the requirements applying at that stage of the debate. The structure of a first Affirmative speech, as it involves special work in definition and subject analysis, will obviously differ from that of any other. A first Negative speech will be constructed somewhat similarly, but basic refutation of the Affirmative case is a special feature which may reduce the amount of development that can be fitted in, especially if definition and interpretation require considerable attention. The next two speeches have similar structure, but second Affirmative may find it expedient to devote considerable time to rebuttal if he faces a stern task in recovering the initiative. The plan of the last two speeches is much the same, but third Affirmative has to allow time to deal with specific points raised by second Negative. Speech structure, then, can be determined in outline by speakers' duties but needs to be varied to suit occasion.

Distribution of time is an aspect of method. The time given to any task can't be decided without consideration of the subject, particularly if it requires more interpretation than most, and the state of conflict. How time is divided among several points is a matter of their relative importance, but it should be remembered that too much time devoted to one item reduces the amount available for others, and that too little time spent on important items reduces the effectiveness of the case.

Proper sequence of argument requires points to be arranged in the order best suited to the team's case. It needn't be chronological order, where that's possible, but it's amateurish to spend time on the present, if the subject relates to that, and then begin delving into the past. There's much to be said for building argument from less significant to more significant points, as this allows the case to grow in stature and may be expected to make the other team's task grow in difficulty. Footholds should be denied to the opposition by establishing logical links between successive points and tying them to the team's line. When these links are welded together to form a chain of argument, the latter will often show remarkable resistance to attack.

The matter-method combination is a union of argument and tactics. To attain the greatest emphasis on conflict, no argument should be planned or used without regard to the difficulties it may be expected to create for the other side, and no argument or rebuttal from the other side is heard without consideration of how it may be refuted and, if possible, advantage secured from it. If it's assumed, reasonably, that there's little to choose in manner or matter between two competent teams, the debate will probably be won by whichever team uses its matter to greater advantage in terms of conflict, or, to put it another way, makes better use of tactics.

Importance of manner

Just as good manner won't sell a poor case, poor manner won't sell a good case. No matter how much merit there is in a speaker's argument, it won't seem so if he fails to present it in such a way as to ensure attention. If he can't get the audience with him he's bound to suffer loss of confidence and his overall level of performance will fall away. This may well have an unsettling effect on the team's succeeding speakers.

Manner has been discussed at length in Chapter 2, and what may be termed its vocal aspects in Chapter 3. Everything which applies to manner and use of voice in public speaking applies with equal force in debating. Debaters and their coaches are therefore advised to make themselves thoroughly familiar with the information set out in those two chapters.

Personality, however, is such a key part of debating manner as to deserve additional treatment here. Projection of personality may well be of greater concern to debaters than to public speakers. Debaters enjoy a time allowance roughly half as much again as competition public speakers and are therefore engaged so much longer in communicating with an audience. The crucial factor is that debaters are constantly taken up with argument, which involves trying to gain and hold audience support, whereas public speakers, though at times they may be required to argue a case, are more likely to have the less demanding task of merely talking about things. To the public speaker personality is largely an agreeable extension of himself, but to the debater it's always a valuable weapon to be used in a combat situation.

In employing his personality to maximum advantage, a debater should make as little use of notes as possible or, if he can manage, not depend on them at all. Unless he gives them only an occasional glance they break his eye contact with the audience, inhibit the expression of his personality, and create a sense of artificiality instead of involvement. He can't convey a feeling of the urgency of what he says if he has to check up at intervals on what he's supposed to be saying or is to say next. Should he doubt his ability to cover enough ground without referring to notes, he's trying to cover too much.

A debater who lacks personality may acquire it without much trouble. He needs a reasonable knowledge of his case, a grasp of debating technique, a dash of self-confidence, a sprinkling of personal charm, a generous portion of sincerity, and a large slice of determination to make people accept his point of view. He mustn't be depressed by the performance of debaters who seem to have an easy proficiency which he'd only like to have, but should set his jaw and go out and get it for himself.

Errors of matter, manner, and method

Debaters should beware of these. None on its own is likely to bring defeat, but speakers guilty of one are often guilty of others. All are beginners' blemishes, despite the fact that many are used by public figures for the express purpose of deception. A combination of the matter and method errors may be expected to delight opposition hearts and make the chance of victory remote.

Common matter errors, including some notable errors of reasoning, are as follows:
- re-stating the subject instead of proving it;
- statements of belief;
- shifts of theme;
- irrelevancies;
- false analogies;
- dependence on trivialities;
- attacking the person instead of his argument;
- confusing words with things;
- unnecessary use of quotations;
- failure to understand "is";
- the "history student's error".

No matter how often or how emphatically a debater re-states the proposition (minus the word "that") during his speech, he isn't proving it by doing so. Perhaps he has fallen for the advertising spiel, "You don't have to prove a thing". It's a trick of demagogues to dispense with proper evidence and repeat a key statement at regular intervals with the idea of fooling people into accepting it. If something is to be re-stated every two minutes it ought to be the team's line.

It's worth nothing for a team to declare its belief in the proposition. All kinds of people believe in all sorts of things. What's needed is proof. While one team is busy with its belief, the other is preparing evidence to show the belief is wrongly founded.

Shifts of theme are usually the result of untidy preparation or of pressure from the other side. If a second speaker's argument can't be readily squared with that of his first speaker, the third has an unenviable task in trying to find common ground. Should one team be driven into a corner by the other, it's at least more dignified to stick to the line and remain there resolutely than to abandon it and be chased from one awkward position to another.

Irrelevancies may be pieces of a prepared case which have been left behind by developments in the debate, or points which a speaker likes so much that he uses them without thought of whether they serve his purpose, or results of muddled thinking. "If it doesn't help the case, don't use it."

Analogies are a useful form of comparison only when they're closely drawn. Validity of inference depends on strictness of parallel. It's sound to argue that writing a novel differs from writing a short story in the same way that speaking for an hour differs from speaking for five minutes, but not to attack popular election of Parliament on the ground that pupils are not competent to choose their teachers.

Trivialities are just that, and to introduce them into a debate is to waste time which should be employed in furthering the argument.

Attacking the person instead of his argument is the *ad hominem* fallacy which has long been a stock weapon of rabble rousers. It's impossible to refute an argument by talking disrespectfully of whoever has advanced it. If the point itself isn't refuted it holds the field, no matter who made it or what sort of person he may be.

Confusing words with things is a sign of sloppy thinking or an intention to deceive. Words are not arguments. It's idle to use such terms as "fascist", "university-controlled tests", and "forces of reaction". Coloured or emotional words are the province of persons who want to draw a conclusion without bothering to produce evidence for it, and as such are beneath the dignity of debaters.

Quotations need to be brief to have point, but are probably better not used. An argument gains no merit because someone else once thought of it, and may be unsound despite that. It's not the quoted authority who has a fight on his hands. Debaters who won't quit quoting excessively will quickly find that such a quantity of quotes will quit them of victory quite tellingly.

Failure to understand "is" (or "are") often leads to trouble. The word "is" in a subject may refer to the immediate present, to a period of some years over which present conditions have existed, or to a continuous present (which may include the foreseeable future) when there's a constant factor. A reasonable meaning for "is", should it occur in the subject, must be established.

The *"history student's error"*, common in senior school debating, is to make a deduction about the present from something which happened in the past without first showing that conditions are still basically the same. History isn't bound to repeat itself.

Common manner errors (excluding what are mere opposites of the positive aspects of manner) are:
● careless deportment;
● negative personality;
● over-positive personality;
● excessive use of slang.

Careless deportment is carrying casualness, pleasant enough in moderation, to an extreme. Nobody is impressed by a speaker who lounges, puts a hand in his pocket, crosses and uncrosses his legs, or fiddles with things. Credibility can't be achieved without some air of authority, and these things destroy that air.

Negative personality likewise detracts from authority. This may be due to nervousness or to a speaker's failure to realise the need to sound as if he's in earnest. Nervousness may be overcome if he takes several deep breaths and concentrates on carrying out the duties of his position, while vigour can be conjured up by sensing the need to secure favourable audience response.

Over-positive personality is a source of annoyance to listeners, who resent being dominated. Truculence, loudness, ridicule of the other side, and flippancy turn them off when it's necessary that they should be turned on. Audience support is quickly lost, and the other team, if its efforts are better controlled, may easily gain a more sympathetic hearing.

Excessive use of slang, a feature of some school debates, is evidence of carelessness which, while it may please the undiscerning, will invite the disapproval of those persons whose support is worth having. The distinction between agreeable colloquialism and cheap slang can be drawn without much trouble.

Common method errors are foolish forecasts, careless conclusions, allocation failures, misplaced development, doing things in the wrong order, undertime, and overtime.

It's amateurish for first Affirmative to forecast that his team will destroy the Negative case (which is yet unheard), or for a third speaker to announce that he has completed the destruction of the other case. It's silly to create an anti-climax by following a persuasive peroration with "Thank you". It's unfair to the other team, and doesn't impress the adjudicator, if a first speaker omits his allocation; shows inexperience if a share of the case is given to third Affirmative; and suggests poor planning if aspects are given to the first two speakers without care having been taken to establish the importance of those aspects.

Loss of method marks can be guaranteed when any speaker returns to one of his earlier points because he has thought of something else to say about it, when third Affirmative adds fresh development at the end of his speech through having unexpected and unwarranted time on his hands, or when any speaker beyond first Affirmative puts the cart before the horse by arguing or summarising his own case before dealing with the case occupying the field. Method marks are also lost for undertime, normally taken as failure to reach the warning bell, and to a greater extent for overtime beyond a half-minute, as answering additional points places an extra burden on the other side. If overtime is simply failure to reach a conclusion, this is poor planning and marks will be deducted for that reason.

During the debate

Before first Affirmative is invited to open the debate, we can imagine the two teams sitting each with its captain in the centre where he can readily discuss matters with both his colleagues. During the opening speech the Negative members should be closely following what's being said, discussing how it affects their prepared case and in what way they may be able to seize the initiative. While first Negative is speaking, the Affirmative members need to consider what effect he's having on the case to which they're now committed. During second Affirmative's speech the Negative should observe closely the extent to which the Affirmative is re-establishing its case and to agree on action to redress the situation.

Whether the issue of the debate has been resolved when second

Affirmative sits down (as it often is) or not, the activities of both teams during the remaining three speeches shouldn't be difficult to imagine. It's worth pointing out that a debater still assists his team after he has spoken, and that a fourth member, if present, should have a set duty, preferably to note points made by the other side and prepare replies to them. And it's a point of etiquette that preparation during the debate should be carried out quietly to avoid distracting the other team.

CHAPTER SEVEN

How To Train Debaters

A debating coach, if he is to succeed, must work just as hard at being a coach as he expects his team to work at being debaters. He must learn all he can about debating and about coaching techniques, and keep learning while he coaches. He must be able to dissociate himself from the contest while it's taking place, and afterwards explain to his debaters how and why they debated well or poorly, and precisely how to improve. He must know how to demonstrate what he wants them to do, and how to inspire them. It isn't necessary for him to have had experience as a debater, though it's helpful unless it has given him ideas which broader experience would have led him to discard. His personality should be agreeable and authoritative, and he needs to project it just as he expects his debaters to project theirs. They should be moved to draw the moral that the approach he has used to convince them is the one they can use to convince others.

A coach of school teams must always offer encouragement. Debaters who haven't reached the final stages of extensive competitions don't really know how proficient they are or what is their probable limit of performance, and may fall away when they could so easily go forward to higher things. The coach should be able to assess their potential with much greater accuracy than they can, and then encourage them to attain it.

An introduction both to public speaking and debating should be made in schools in Year 7, if it hasn't already been made at upper primary level. The English syllabus operates from Year 7 with oral expression as an increasingly important part of it, and debating gives special point to that expression. As every teacher knows, it's much easier to generate enthusiasm for a new intellectual activity in Year 7 than later. As every coach knows, the sooner debaters are given a chance to develop their skill the more of it they're likely to develop. When they reach competitive debating at about Year 10, they will already possess a valuable background of experience. On the other hand, debaters have been successfully introduced to the art in Year 11 or as adults, but in such instances satisfaction may depend on the ability to learn useful techniques quickly.

Selecting a junior team

Before a debating team can be trained, its members have to be chosen. After first briefly explaining the basic techniques of public speaking and of preparing and presenting a simple debating case, the coach should test candidates by instant debating, as explained earlier (Chapter 4), with an Affirmative and Negative speech by each candidate. If two minutes' maximum is allowed each speaker, there's little problem in giving a provisional grading to most candidates, who are then placed in teams thought to be roughly equal in merit. Two or more teams are selected from graded candidates, coached in technique, assisted in preparation of cases, and given two or three debates, with a limit of four minutes per speaker.

Placing the three members of a team is a matter of matching personal qualifications with those required for the various positions. A first speaker should be able to interpret the subject and explain the team's line. A third speaker needs the ability to grasp the essentials of the other team's case, summarise his own, and compare the two to his team's advantage. A second speaker depends less on specialised ability and often has more scope for use of personality. In terms of all-round debating skill the third speaker is often the best, followed by the first speaker. If their abilities seem equal, they can change positions during the year and so broaden their experience.

Need for precise training

Once debaters have been initiated into their art they have to be trained. It's no good letting them flounder along on the win-some-lose-some principle or competition against growing numbers of trained teams may lead them to flounder along on the win-none-lose-all principle, which is damaging to morale. If a thing is to be done it ought to be well done, for there lies satisfaction. Besides, young debaters may want to reach the top of the tree, even if it's only a local one. Some of them may want to climb higher trees. The sooner they learn correct techniques the better chance they have of progressing fast and far.

It's easy to say that coaches simply have to instruct their debaters in how to prepare and present a case (Chapters 5-6). That's perfectly true, but it can't be done all at once. The amount and kind of instruction must be related to age and general ability.

But the emphasis from the outset at any level must be on communication and conflict.

Practice in instant debating comes first, for this is the quickest and surest way of bringing out what each speaker has. He learns to think quickly and positively, to speak to a theme, and to use his personality as the key factor in conveying a sense of conviction. He learns not to depend on notes, and to be concise.

As personality is so important to communication, coaches should assess each debater's personality with a view to improving strengths and eliminating weaknesses. That's always the correct order, for an aspiring debater needs to feel he's doing more of the right things than merely fewer of the wrong ones. And it's a matter of checking his personality against its various aspects as described earlier (Chapter 2) and then setting to work. However, it's unwise to risk the unsettling effect of an extensive change of personality, and it may be sufficient for the coach to promote warmth and sincerity.

Coaching in preparation of cases

Key words and phrases should be encountered at once, for it's almost impossible to keep them out of subjects. An early meeting with complexity in a modified form is advisable, for the most innocent-looking subjects sometimes have tigers crouching behind them.

Two simple subjects ("That we should slow down" and "That saying it is better than writing it") are used here to show the kind of instruction a coach needs to give. Each is studied from definition and subject analysis to suitable Affirmative and Negative cases, with some emphasis on denial of opportunities to the other side.

"That we should slow down":
"We" needs to be related to "slow down". Are "we" people who ride bikes or drive cars, those living in the debaters' town or district, persons of their age group, or all human beings? In what sense are they going fast? Does "should" suggest moral obligation or just a very good idea? By looking at the possible meanings of simple words and fixing a broad area of debate it's reasonable to take "we" as members of urbanised societies whose pace of living is fast, "should" as suggesting a good idea, and "slow down" as "reduce the pace of living". The total meaning given allows a wider and more useful area of debate than if definitions were chosen to support the overall meaning that we, as car drivers, ought to observe speed limits.

The next step is to use this complete definition as the basis for an Affirmative case. It's a matter of asking "Why?", or perhaps "How?" It helps greatly if the answer gives two clear and strong reasons, each capable of some development. The answer should be checked at once to see whether it invites a strong Negative reply. If it does, it must be rejected in favour of one which doesn't.

Why should we slow down? Why is it a good idea for us as members of urbanised societies to reduce the pace of our living? Two clear and strong reasons come to mind. We should do so because we suffer physically and mentally from being in a rat-race, and because we don't give ourselves time to enjoy the peace and quiet which life can hold for us. The first two speakers should have no trouble in dealing with one reason each, and neither reason offers an obvious Negative foothold.

As debates lost by Affirmatives are commonly lost through case weakness, particularly if the Negative can exploit that weakness, the coach should warn his debaters against ways in which, when Affirmative, they may scuttle themselves. To argue that we should slow down because otherwise we'll exhaust ourselves invites a Negative attack based on the ground that coping with the growing pace of life has increased our power of endurance. To argue that we should slow down because it takes less effort is invalid, as nobody can deny it.

The coach should give his team practice in the Negative approach. An obvious difference between skilled and unskilled teams is that the latter don't like being Negative, whereas the skilled ones rejoice at the opportunities which the Negative position usually brings with it. At first the coach shouldn't concern his debaters with the four standard Negative approaches but, after warning them against an invalid Negative, should encourage them to look, even if sometimes vainly, for a case with more scope than the simple Negative. In each instance he should outline an Affirmative case and invite suggestions for a two-division Negative case to answer the question "Why shall we oppose this view?"

To oppose the Affirmative case previously given for "That we should slow down" (physical and mental strain; no time to enjoy peace and quiet), he may settle for a simple Negative one that we should match the pace of life because we'd be left behind otherwise and because it provides the kind of challenge needed to save us from boredom. To the question "How would you first refute the Affirmative case?" he should accept the answer that we can overcome strain by learning to accommodate it and that we can make time at week-ends to enjoy peace and quiet.

"That saying it is better than writing it":
Careful definition is needed for "saying", "writing", and "better". Does "saying" cover use of television, radio, and recording? Does "writing" cover printing and therefore printed material? "Better" in what way and for whom? Does "is" refer only to the present time, or to all time?

If "better" is taken as "more effective", saying it versus writing it becomes a question of relative impact, both being effective but one more so. A useful break-up would feature immediate impact as an advantage, coupled with the special power of speech to express personality. The Negative could gain nothing from that, and would almost certainly argue in terms of lasting advantage. An Affirmative case which is invalid because there's no answer to it is to argue that saying it is better through being easier.

A Negative case on this one needs to be of the second standard type, showing that the proposition and Affirmative case are not necessarily true. The Negative can show that the Affirmative's short-term argument fails to take account of long-term factors, and then show first that the long view must be taken to obtain proper perspective and next that writing things ensures their endurance long after the spoken word has been forgotten.

The coach's notebook

The other and equally important half of the coach's work is done after each debate, when he reviews his team's performance, discusses any problems encountered, and indicates ways of improvement. To do this effectively he needs a notebook in which to record certain details. Each page should be divided for comment on matter, manner, and method, with space for such additional remarks (perhaps on conflict or use of the initiative) as may seem necessary. Points made by the adjudicator, but not noted by the coach, should be recorded in red, and a coach's comment also made by the adjudicator should be given a red tick. When the debate finishes, but before the adjudication begins, the coach is advised to write one sentence stating which team he believes has won, and why. This allows him to balance his judgment against that of the adjudicator, and this, if the latter is as competent as he should be, is useful to him in his further coaching. But a coach whose verdict differs from that of a competent adjudicator needs to review his own basis of judgment.

The coach's notebook is invaluable as a critical record of performance, and of patterns within performances. Unsatisfactory features have a way of repeating themselves, and notebook information helps the coach to identify and overcome them. Preparation from the notebook of a brief case history of each speaker directs attention to the strong and weak points of each and allows the former to be used as a base for progress while the latter are being remedied. The coach whose notebook is a useful part of his equipment can expect to be rewarded by his team's enthusiastic co-operation.

Until a debater has attained considerable skill there will be many areas in which improvement is desirable. It's the coach's business to know them all, but to concentrate on no more than two or three at a time. In this way he doesn't ask a speaker to attack many problems at once, and noticeable progress may be expected. The steady improvement which each debater is likely to show boosts team morale. And, though a speaker may fall into some fresh errors, his overall standard of performance is bound to improve through his progressive avoidance of previous ones.

Working with senior teams

All debaters from the beginning of Year 11 (including those who take up the art as adults) as well as outstanding younger ones, should study the seven kinds of subjects and four standard Negative approaches described in Chapter 5, for knowing how to turn these matters to advantage greatly assists performance at senior school level and upwards. While subjects for senior debating may be of any type, most are likely to concern the truth of the proposition or to require interpretation, and key words and comparisons are often thrown in for good measure. Comparisons may be implied without the use of a comparative word, simply because two things are presented for discussion at the one time.

With senior teams the coach is recommended to take a selection of subjects of the more difficult kinds, discuss their possible meanings with his team, and then consider Affirmative and Negative cases, including Negatives to offset declared Affirmatives. Obviously the standard Negative approaches must be examined before this can be done effectively.

Handling of truth-of-proposition subjects

In "That tradition is the enemy of progress" the key word is a strong one, "enemy". Thought must be given to the kind of action taken by an enemy, the extent of tradition, and the nature of progress. Can there be a new tradition, can one man's idea of progress be the opposite of another's, and is there then some chance of preparing a case to take the Negative by surprise?

In "That we have a duty to be provocative" the argument turns on "duty" (another strong word) and "provocative". Is there something to be made of the fact that strike leaders who provoke community hostility now describe threatened action against themselves as "provocative"? Would the Affirmative do well to argue a duty to take so-called provocative action against people and groups who act provocatively to advance sectional interests?

In "That democracy is in danger" the Affirmative has almost too much scope. What is democracy? What does danger imply? Is it in danger from the Right, the Left, both of them, from militant unions, from Governments of whatever complexion which would act against them, from the masses which are too apathetic to defend it?

Handling of interpretation subjects

"That faded jeans are to be worn with pride" suggests that people should be proud to identify themselves with a certain age-group by wearing clothes which are accepted as a badge of the group. "That to the man in the middle, life is a riddle" refers to a familiar meat-in-the-sandwich, don't-know-whether-I'm-coming-or-going situation. "That fine words butter no parsnips" may mean "mere protestations do not alter facts" (Oxford) or perhaps be another way of saying that flattery gets us nowhere.

The coach should warn his team of the danger lurking in subjects which are non-debatable if taken literally. They may contain an absolute which happens to be a popular exaggeration. Such an absolute is "never" in the subjects "That you never can tell" and "That you never know your luck". They may express a contradiction, as in "That you can have it both ways" and "That happiness is no laughing matter". They may be patently obvious, like "That we should begin at the beginning" or "That women are female". They may be of doubtful truth, like "That penny plain is twopence coloured" or "That the Affirmative deserves to win". But all of them must be taken in a debatable sense, even if careful cogitation is called for.

The coach must make his team understand "That you never can tell", for example, probably means, in a debating sense, that life has many surprises (the Negative reply perhaps being that if we take the trouble we can at least foresee the possibility of most things happening). "That happiness is no laughing matter" suggests the need for serious application if happiness is to be created and spread around. "That women are female" could put the view that women react in terms of their sex. "That the Affirmative deserves to win" can be presented as a plea for positive thinking.

General advice

Solid work should be done on the standard Negative approaches (Chapter 5), especially the second and fourth kinds ("not necessarily true" and change of direction) in view of their usefulness in putting pressure on an Affirmative committed to a particular line. The "not generally true" approach is applicable in almost every instance. This means that the first approach (simple Negative, or "not true") need be adopted only when there seems no scope for the second, while the third (proving the converse) or fourth are worth consideration when the Affirmative case suggests it and the Negative team feels like using the thumb screws.

The coach should deter his team from engaging in a battle of examples. It's quite possible for the Affirmative to support its case with a set of sound illustrations, while the Negative case is supported with a different set of sound illustrations. But, to play an effective part in a debate, examples must be tied to an argument showing the superiority of one case over the other.

Regular practice is just as necessary for debaters as for any other persons engaged in competitive activity. First-class competition performance can't be expected without prior match practice, and form can't be held over a lengthy break without match practice. It's the coach's responsibility to secure this practice, either by debates within a club or school or by social debates against outside teams. The social debate, especially if it's a mixed-sexes affair followed by afternoon tea or supper, is also useful in promoting debating as a pleasant cultural activity. Adult teams seeking pre-competition practice, or a stiff contest before competing at a higher level, shouldn't overlook the possibilities offered in some States by leading school teams.

When a practice debate within a school is only possible with teams of unequal strength, it's worthwhile changing their composition to achieve a rough equality. This offers juniors the chance to learn from working with seniors. If only the three team members and a reserve are available for practice, a pairs debate is indicated. If it's simply a case of the three debaters, the coach may dispense with formal adjudications (which he'd give otherwise) and make a fourth for pairs or even turn himself into a one-person team and give three speeches. It's important that he should be prepared to demonstrate how a task should be performed.

Debaters who think purposefully about debating may be expected to perform with greater consistency. This kind of thinking among school debaters can be fostered by the partial use of seniors to train juniors and to adjudicate junior debates. It eases the coach's burden and has particular value in concentrating the senior debaters' minds on fundamentals and match-winning techniques. And it's interesting to observe the eager attention given by juniors to seniors who've reached the heights they hope to attain themselves.

Instant debating, previously mentioned (Chapter 4), is a valuable coaching device. It trains debaters to think quickly and concisely, to communicate without hesitation, and to use personality to advantage. Experience in it protects them from that loss of confidence otherwise often produced by the need to prepare an entirely new case while the debate is in progress. Shrewd coaches have been known to resort to it as a means of curing over-confidence brought on by easy victories.

Debaters shouldn't be expected to perform indefinitely in a vacuum. They can learn little of advanced techniques, and can scarcely comprehend the performance levels of splendidly competent debaters, if the only other debaters they meet are of similar standard to themselves. At a stage when they're best equipped to learn from what they see and hear, they should be given an opportunity to observe skilled debaters in action. If they live in cities where adult debating is of good standard, their coach should ensure that they see something of the better teams. If they live in country areas where debating is largely confined to schools, it should be arranged that they attend finals of schools' State-wide or similar competitions.

Exhibitions in country centres allow local debaters to observe talented visitors in action without having to travel to a capital city for the purpose. These have most successfully featured outstanding school teams in displays of team, singles, and instant debating. When each segment is prefaced by a brief account of what to look for, and followed by a quick expert adjudication, audience interest is heightened even further and valuable lessons are readily absorbed.

Seminars provide a useful means of collecting information on various aspects of debating. A week-end seminar has long been held early each year in one capital city, and the idea should have been copied. There's nothing to stop anyone from arranging one anywhere, but it will only be as useful as the invited speakers and the programme permit. Speakers, irrespective of their debating experience, must have made a thorough study of the principles and techniques of the art. The programme needs to cover preparation and presentation of a case and the skills of adjudication, and include a session for questions from the audience. A recommended addition is an annotated debate, in which, after first Affirmative has spoken, each team is shut away in turn before its next speech, while an adjudicator comments to the audience on the situation at that stage and outlines the courses open to the following speaker.

In a school it's the coach's privilege to promote debating. He needs students to keep coming forward to be trained, for otherwise the art will die out when current performers leave or, as sometimes happens, abandon it under the mistaken impression that it interferes with studies, when of course it assists in developing and maintaining a logical and critical approach. So there must be debates in which students may take part from junior to senior level, and which numbers of students may attend and enjoy. Lunchtime competitions are an obvious possibility, with subjects possessing strong popular appeal. Students should be encouraged to take part in parliamentary debates, inside and outside classes. Team, pairs and singles competitions, at junior and senior levels, are worth conducting within the school to encourage development of skills and to increase audience interest. As many competitions as possible should be entered in order to provide debaters with wide and varied opportunities, and sights should be set high rather than low in order to gain experience and satisfaction from staying part of the course, or maybe all of it, at a higher level.

Training school debaters isn't the sort of job that can be fitted into the odd half-hour in a 9 a.m. to 3.30 p.m. day. It requires the constant and imaginative concentration expected of the debaters themselves. It's not a job for anyone who lacks self-discipline and who places great emphasis on material reward. It's a job for persons who appreciate the worth of showing others how to argue convincingly.

CHAPTER EIGHT

How To Adjudicate Debates

Adjudication is just as much an art as public speaking and debating. It can't be carried out successfully by persons who haven't studied its particular techniques. Unless precise methods of evaluation are laid down and required to be followed, each adjudicator is likely to make his own, which may differ significantly from those of others. This means that a team which wins decisively with one adjudicator may lose no less decisively with another. Debaters will then be disheartened, coaches infuriated, and adjudication brought into contempt.

Adjudicators, if they are to give decisions which will command respect, must follow the guidelines set out in this chapter. These are accepted by the Australian Debating Federation, its member bodies (the State Debating Unions), and the New South Wales Department of Education — that is, by the principal debating organisations in Australia. The guidelines form the basic content of Australia's only training course for adjudicators, that which is conducted each year on behalf of the New South Wales Department of Education for candidates for appointment.

Coaches and debaters are also recommended to study this chapter. They should know the basis on which decisions are reached by adjudicators. And they should equip themselves for any adjudication they may be called on to perform as part of their normal activities.

Nobody, of course, can hope to make a sound assessment of debating performance without a clear understanding of the principles of debating. Preceding chapters should be read now if this hasn't already been done, and, in particular, the techniques of preparing and presenting a case (Chapters 5-6) should be studied closely.

Principles of adjudication

It must be emphasised that, though debating is communication as well as conflict, and manner skills are of great assistance in enthralling an audience and enlisting support for an argument, the team which wins the conflict of argument may reasonably expect to win the debate. Superior manner, so attractive and so potent in swaying audiences which don't understand that a team's chief object is to win an argument, isn't often a deciding factor unless the battle of wits is either closely or indifferently fought.

However, as stated previously, reading of speeches and serious undertime may change the situation. And a team's considerable manner superiority, by no means rare, may properly be held sufficient to win the debate if it has reasonably applied itself to conflict without getting the better of that conflict. Life, for adjudicators, wasn't meant to be easy, though mostly it's comparatively so.

Adjudicators must have a clear appreciation of the importance of the initiative in debating. They should look for its use by all speakers after first Affirmative, and be alert to chart its progress from side to side.

There are three initiative points to remember:

● if there's little or no conflict, the initiative hasn't moved (it's still in the initial stage), and the Affirmative has a claim to victory because its case hasn't been disputed;

● if the Negative seizes the initiative, and the Affirmative does little or nothing about recapturing it, or does something but fails to achieve its object, the Negative retains the initiative and is likely to win the debate;

● if the Affirmative succeeds in regaining the initiative from first Negative, an Affirmative victory may be expected.

That's often where the battle ends, for the Negative, through its second speaker, is rarely able to capture the initiative a second time. If it does achieve this, the battle may be strongly contested by both third speakers. When that happens, the outcome probably won't be clear until some time during the final speech, or, infrequently, not until the very end.

An adjudicator should simplify his task by first getting the Affirmative line clear in his mind. He must then note what the Negative does with it, and secure a clear picture of the Negative line. After that he needs to watch for the Affirmative's reply to the Negative case. The only difficulty which may confront him during the first two speeches is to work out a team line if a first speaker omits to state it precisely.

If the debate is a cliff-hanger (though few debates really are), third Negative's performance may decide the issue. If it's not particularly close before he speaks, often because his first two speakers haven't engaged in serious conflict, it's unreasonable to regard his performance as having pulled things round. He may well be posting his letter after the box has been cleared.

A special warning. Adjudicators are most certainly *not entitled* to use their judgment of the merits of a case as the basis for a decision. It's improper for them to take into account any preference they may have for one case rather than the other because it has greater coherence, is logically superior, or expresses their own feelings in the matter. A debate is between Affirmative and Negative, not between the adjudicator and Affirmative or Negative. The Affirmative case, for example, may be ill-devised, lacking in coherence, and poorly developed, it may stumble from one assertion to another, but if the Negative is so witless as to let it stand, there it will stand, and it will still win the debate for the Affirmative.

Victory must never be declared on grounds which are themselves debatable. The image of debating will be tarnished if the official debate is followed by an unofficial one on the subject of the adjudicator's competence. It's wholly unreasonable to award victory for some minor reason (such as slight undertime or overtime, poor deportment, rather much colloquialism), on a subjective point (such as personal dislike of arguments used), or for punitive reasons. Unsatisfactory etiquette can be effectively dealt with by a verbal flaying of offenders.

How to record details

An adjudicator is recommended to use a book to record details of each debate. This allows him to compare the notes he makes on different occasions and the marks he gives, and to establish a pattern of written comment. It's helpful whenever he's asked for his impressions of certain debaters whom he has judged.

Three double pages should be used for each debate. Details of first Affirmative's and first Negative's speeches are entered on the first double page, the left page being used for the Affirmative (as that team sits on the adjudicator's left, though on the chairman's right) and the right page for the Negative. Details of later speeches are also recorded on double pages.

There's no need to divide a page in any way, but it's usual to enter marks across the foot, leaving room to alter them as required, and to leave space for any brief manner and method comments just above the marks. With the speaker's name across the top (prefaced by A1, N1, A2, N2, A3, or N3 to indicate side and position), most of the page is clear for notes on matter and the course of conflict. Above the speaker's name on the first page the words of the subject and team names should be written.

The rule for note-making is to put down nothing but essentials, but not to omit any essentials. As the adjudicator has to observe speakers' manner and audience rapport, he can't write at length. It's helpful to use ticks, crosses, question-marks, block letters, and underlinings for various purposes, and to have a set of abbreviations to cover most contingencies. A, N, KW, EC, TM, TL, R, ALL, n, nn, np, DEF, G, RH, LH, IN, CC are a batch taken at random from one book and standing respectively for Affirmative, Negative, key word, eye contact, too much, too little, refutation, allocation, notes, no notes, note pause, definition, gesture, right hand, left hand, initiative, and comparison of cases. Arrows can be used to link points, especially from one page to its opposite, while an upward or downward arrow after the letters EC indicates eye contact with ceiling or floor instead of audience.

When the adjudicator is recording first Affirmative, he'll need to note definition, subject analysis, line, and allocation (the latter in two lines, for A1 and A2). It's usually sufficient to jot down a basic item about every minute, but it's necessary to show the development of the argument. Actual words may sometimes be thought worth noting. Critical comments should be entered at the side, in block letters, so that they may be seen at a glance when the speech is being evaluated.

Recording first Negative follows a similar pattern, but definition and interpretation call for noting only so far as some difference emerges. As the question of the initiative now arises, brief notes, preferably in block letters, must refer to it. It's also advisable to note details of any Negative failure to come to terms with the Affirmative case. All these matters will have to be given critical mention in the adjudication, and the adjudicator needs to be precise about them.

The note plan for each side's second speaker may now be imagined, with an important comment on the position of the initiative after second Affirmative's speech. Care is required in making notes on the two third speakers in view of the fact that, with the possible but undesirable exception of third Affirmative, they are not developing the argument but comparing the two cases. It's easy to write very little about them and later be faced with the problem of talking freely about them. A workable plan is to note the chief points both of comparison and refutation, and to label them with ticks or crosses. A short sentence near the foot of the third Negative page should state the reason for awarding the debate to whichever side, as it's essential that this be clearly explained in the final part of the adjudication.

Experienced adjudicators often write much less than may be assumed from the above. Some adopt the principle of writing nothing which doesn't assist the overall evaluation, scattering some block-letter words around, getting by with ticks, crosses, question-marks, underlinings, and arrows wherever they can, and remembering always that it pays to be precise. An adjudicator should aim to develop a pattern of note-making which seems best suited to him, as his competence won't be judged by what he writes but by his decisions and how he justifies them.

Judging matter, manner, and method

The various aspects of matter, manner, and method were discussed previously (Chapters 2 and 6), but are re-stated here for convenience. Adjudicators should form a general impression of each, and never attempt the hair-splitting, time-consuming process of weighing various alleged aspects of every one of the three.

Judging matter is judging argument, what led up to it, and what follows from it. Consideration must be given to its clarity, relevance, reasonableness, weight, and development, to freedom from errors of reasoning, and use of illustration. All the adjudicator can do about faulty argument is to mark it down, remembering that it may yet win the debate if it isn't contested. He mustn't be influenced by any special knowledge he possesses, but must look at arguments from the viewpoint of the "average reasonable man".

Judging manner calls for awareness of five things. These are:
● eye contact with the audience (also involving limited or no use of notes);
● deportment and gesture (with stress on naturalness);
● use of language (good conversational English, at a level suitable to subject and occasion, with effective opening, intermediate passages, and ending);
● use of voice (articulation, flow of words, pleasantness, variation in pàce-pitch-tone-volume, use of pause);
● projection of personality.

Judgment of manner can be somewhat subjective, with one adjudicator finding strong appeal in A1 but not N1, and another finding it the other way round. It's well to steer a middle course, weighing the various parts of manner as objectively as possible. While an adjudicator is quite entitled to award a debate on manner, he should be satisfied that a manner advantage for one team isn't outweighed by an advantage for the other in terms of conflict.

Judging method is straightforward, as it concerns only the structure of a speech and its worth as part of a team case. Structure is the orderly arrangement of material, logical progression from point to point, and the giving of suitable time and emphasis to each part. Organisation to fit the team case, both beforehand and as may be necessary during the debate, should suit a speaker's position in the team and strike the right balance between arguing one case and refuting the other.

Marking of speeches

An adjudicator must never add up his marks in order to discover which team has won the debate. He must first decide the winner and then total his marks, making such adjustments as may be necessary to reflect his decision. Experienced adjudicators usually relate marks continually to a changing situation, so that when the last speaker resumes his seat the marks at once indicate the final state of the debate.

The same range of marks is necessarily used for speeches at any level of performance, for otherwise marks would give no indication of ability at that level. The interstate adult debater who performs well may expect a 75-80 score, and so may the junior debater who performs well at his much lower level. Neither of them, no matter how well he performs, should be given a mark much above 80, for the adjustment of marks which is sometimes necessary to produce a correct result might then produce some absurd individual marks. Besides, what scope for improvement is there for a debater scoring 90 or more? He may even do better next time and, with a different adjudicator or in a different overall situation, obtain a lower mark.

It's a useful convention to regard 75 (made up of 30 for matter, 30 for manner, 15 for method) as a total mark indicating a "good average performance". For a performance well above that standard a mark of 80 might be given, and for one well below it a mark of 70, falling to the 60s where there's clear ignorance of debating technique, such as in reading of speeches or failure to engage in conflict, and to the 50s or under where there's gross undertime. But a very low mark for one speaker may produce a big difference in team totals, and if the teams are close together in terms of conflict that mark will have to be increased. The team which wins obviously needs to be given a higher total, and certain marks may need to be moved upwards to ensure this. The most obvious instance is that of the inferior team which automatically wins because its talented opponents have argued an invalid case and which, despite what may be in itself a poor performance, must receive marks high enough to support victory.

Marks should be relative in all respects. If one speaker gets 30 for matter, any other with better matter should get at least 31, and with poorer matter should drop at least to 29. The same applies with manner and method. Relativity also requires that the team with generally superior matter has the higher matter total, and likewise with manner and method.

The overall position, as well as relative merit, must be clear from the marking. The team in possession of the initiative at the end of the debate is entitled to higher totals in both parts of the matter-method combination, and its matter-method margin must offset any higher manner total for the other side. First Negative's total, if he has captured the initiative, should exceed that of first Affirmative by at least one mark. If second Affirmative regains the initiative, this can only be shown by giving him a total at least one mark above that for first Negative. In constructing a total mark for each speaker, the adjudicator must therefore see it in the perspective of the whole debate. This is still possible if he fixes a speaker's total before deciding what three marks will produce it.

It's proper to reduce a speaker's mark for undertime or overtime, for otherwise there's no advantage in tailoring a speech, as some debaters do very well, to fit a time allowance. The normal practice is to deduct one method mark when the speech finishes just after the warning bell, and two or more method marks when the warning bell isn't reached. It's usually one off for a half-minute over, and two or more off when overtime exceeds one minute, overtime being more serious in that, except when indulged in by third Negative, it increases the other debating team's burden of reply.

Serious undertime, such as speaking for perhaps half the permitted time or even less, requires a reduction in all three of matter, manner, and method, for adequate opportunity hasn't been given to assess the general standard of performance. It's quite wrong to hold that a good short speech deserves a good mark, for adjudicators are not entitled to assume the standard would have been maintained if the speech had run full time. But the necessary result of the debate must be regarded as an over-riding factor, and undertime may escape some of its penalty in order that overall justice may be done.

Debaters mustn't be penalised for errors for which they can't be held responsible, such as faulty timekeeping, the chairman's failure to announce the subject, or for being thrown off balance by unforeseen interruptions, external noise, or the reactions of a partisan audience. The adjudicator should halt the debate to make an important timekeeping correction or for any other reason he considers sufficient, and then allow certain recovery time. Some of these problems are better prevented, and a thoughtful adjudicator will make a pre-debate check of subject and speaking times both with the teams and the chairman and will check bell times himself during the debate.

No adjudicator should make a noticeable contribution to dead time during a debate. An audience is never stimulated by the sight of him poring over his notes for a minute or more between speeches, and for an even longer time after the sixth speech. Experienced adjudicators, unless surprised by an early ending, are able to signal the chairman to call the next speaker immediately the previous one has sat down, and are ready to take the floor at the end without delay. The secret is to enter a speaker's marks, and to cease making notes, before he has finished speaking. Relative checking of marks, and any necessary alteration to them, is carried on all the time, and totals are entered and checked for accuracy before the debate ends. A short delay is excusable only after the fifth or sixth speeches, and then only if there's a cliffhanger situation calling for careful review of key factors.

Handling difficult decisions

An adjudicator, if he's to give sound decisions in what may seem difficult situations, having regard for the fact that ties are not permitted, needs to be sensitive to every facet of a debate. This allows a proper reason for the verdict to be established without time being spent in uncomfortably thinking matters over after third Negative has finished.

The following advice should be helpful:

- If manner is roughly equal, the team which wins the argument (by retaining the initiative, or by seizing and holding it), should win the debate unless there's a strong reason (reading of speeches, serious undertime) against it.
- If one team's manner is clearly superior, but it loses the argument, a decision will depend on whether it made a serious effort in argument. This requires a personal decision on how seriously losing the argument should be viewed, but reasonable

evidence has to be produced when the adjudication is being delivered.

- If a third speaker performs poorly in a close situation, it's reasonable to regard inferior performance under test as deciding the issue in favour of the other side.
- If matter, manner, and method are all roughly equal, consideration should be given to establishing a margin in matter or method rather than manner if there's any likelihood that in this instance evaluation of manner will be thought subjective.
- If neither team shows much understanding of the art of debating, the decision should be given in favour of the team which showed a somewhat greater degree of understanding, perhaps by engaging to some extent in conflict, communicating better, pursuing its line more consistently (maybe even having a line to pursue), or making better use of illustration. This may also be a personal decision needing careful support.

Delivering the adjudication

Next comes the adjudication, with teams and audience prepared to hang on every word. If the "seventh speech" is a dull affair, with no projection of any interesting personality, this in-built advantage will be wasted. And if it's a savagely critical affair, with much blasting of speakers whose chief fault is not knowing how to do better, the advantage will still be wasted, as feelings of frustration and annoyance hinder effective listening.

One requirement in every adjudication must be strictly observed: there has to be a clear statement showing why the debate is being awarded to one team and not the other. Without this statement the teams, coaches, and audience will be left to guess the reason, and there can be no certainty of their guessing correctly. Failure to supply this statement may fairly be taken as a sign that the adjudicator is below an acceptable standard. It weakens confidence in adjudicators generally. It's unjust to debaters, who can draw no informed conclusions on what to do next time.

A particularly successful adjudication pattern begins with comments on manner, moves to an analysis of the two cases, the grounds of conflict, and the development of argument and conflict, passes to a precise explanation of how the decision was reached, and ends with that decision. Woven into the fabric is such favourable comment as can be made, whatever re-statement of fundamental debating principles seems necessary, and such advice as may be expected to lead to improved performance. Emphasis is placed on what was required to be done at any stage and how effectively it was done. And there's no mention of marks, though these may be given to debaters on request.

An adjudication shouldn't normally exceed the time allowed for a speaker in the debate. The adjudicator can't cover the required ground in much less time, and if he takes much longer he's either telling the audience things which should be reserved for the debaters or taking unfair advantage of a captive audience. And he should refer only briefly to his notebook, and may even speak without it, if he's to project his personality and maintain that audience contact which he expects of the debaters.

Sometimes the adjudicator may be one of the few persons present with sufficient experience to appreciate debating as a lively art. In such cases he has an opportunity through his comments to explain the merits of debating, to encourage regard for it among audiences which previously had little understanding of the lively possibilities of communication and conflict, and to set ordinary debaters on the road to satisfaction and success. By showing enthusiasm for debating he can do much to promote it in others.

Panel adjudications

For semi-finals and finals it's often the custom to use a panel of three adjudicators (to have five may reflect on their general competence) in order to increase the likelihood that a just decision will be reached. A panel decision may be unanimous or that of a majority. An adjudication is usually delivered on behalf of the panel by one of its members, who should never be the minority part of a 2-1 verdict. In some circles a mere announcement of the result is given, but this is an intolerable practice, for nobody can gain anything from it. As one person can't really put the views of three who've been working separately, the best plan may be for each panel member to give a brief adjudication (the dissenting opinion, if there is one, coming second) in order that three presumably expert judgments may be heard.

Adjudicators' training course

This is an outline of the course devised by the writer and conducted each year for the New South Wales Department of Education for the purpose of having some sixty qualified persons to handle high school competition debates in the Sydney area.

Most candidates are university students in their first or second year who are invited on the basis of a successful school debating record. Nearly all receive appointment on completing the course and become satisfactory adjudicators, some of them performing with distinction after two or three years in the field.

The course is conducted by a senior adjudicator with considerable experience in lecturing on debating principles and techniques and in coaching championship-winning senior school teams. Twenty-four candidates are normally accepted, twelve for each of two courses, but a third course is held if required. Each candidate is given a set of notes to be studied before attending the course, for which six hours are allotted on each of two days.

On the first morning the principles and basic techniques of debating are explained, then the principles and basic techniques of adjudication, excluding delivery of the latter. In the afternoon a senior school debate is held, and candidates make notes and hand in mark-sheets, each containing a brief statement of reasons for the decision. Discussion of the debate is led by the instructor, who raises a wide variety of matters. After a review of what has been covered to that stage he explains and demonstrates the delivery of an adjudication. At the end of the day each candidate receives a sheet of questions on which to test his debating knowledge at home. The instructor takes away the mark-sheets to check each candidate's assessment of the debate.

On the second morning four senior school debates are held at schools near the training centre, three candidates and an examiner (an experienced adjudicator) being allotted to each debate. After the debate each candidate delivers an adjudication in turn without being allowed to hear any before his own. Candidates' mark-sheets, with a brief explanation of the verdict, are given to the instructor for a check based on comparison with examiners' sheets. Each examiner discusses his three candidates' performance with them, offering criticism and advice. After recess the twelve candidates assemble to hear reports from all four examiners.

On the second afternoon the instructor discusses his findings from the two sets of candidates' mark-sheets and verdict statements, with particular comment on any apparent errors of judgment. Candidates are asked to mention any difficulties they found, and these are resolved. Answers to the first day's questions are obtained at random and reinforced as required. Techniques for handling difficult decisions are explained. After a review of the basics of delivering an adjudication, each candidate gives without preparation a selected part of the adjudication of an imaginary debate briefly described by the instructor, who comments on aspects of the performance. The course ends with a general review and any necessary explanation of competition duties.

In the light of experience the course requires extension. The candidate should attend a debate adjudicated by his examiner, complete a mark-sheet (which goes to the instructor with a check-sheet from the examiner), observe the adjudication, and discuss it with the examiner. On a second occasion he should adjudicate a debate in the presence of the course instructor, who, if satisfied with the level of performance, will list him as a Class 2 adjudicator, being thereby qualified to handle zone debates, and, if reports during the season are satisfactory, a limited number of inter-zone (knockout) debates at the organiser's discretion. To become a Class 1 adjudicator, qualified to handle debates without restriction, he should have at least a year's experience, give an acceptable adjudication in the presence of the course instructor, and answer satisfactorily and without notice a number of questions designed to test his reaction to various problems with which he may be faced.

A course of this nature may be organised anywhere and should produce competent adjudicators if a capable instructor is secured and the candidates are of reasonable quality. In fact, it's recommended that efforts be made to establish such a course in any area where considerable interest in debating is being shown. Debating standards will scarcely improve if adjudication leaves something to be desired.

Experience has shown that shortening the course to a one-day format greatly reduces its effectiveness. However, should there seem to be no alternative, in a country area where accommodation may be a factor, the first morning programme (principles and technique of debating and adjudication) must not be reduced. Two or more groups of debates, depending on the number of candidates, would need to be held in the afternoon, with examiners to assist the instructor as required. Candidates should mark their first debate, discuss the debate and their assessments with the instructor or examiner, deliver an adjudication of the second debate, take part in discussion on that, and then listen to a review of the day's proceedings. The question sheets used in the two-day course should be issued, to be sent to the instructor on completion. After that the instructor should report on the candidates' probable capabilities to the local organiser.

Satisfactory performance by a candidate at a course of instruction doesn't automatically make him a competent adjudicator. It simply means that he has acquired the necessary grounding and is likely to make sound judgments. He may be expected to raise his level of performance as he strengthens his foundations with experience.

CHAPTER NINE

Subjects For Debate

Need for subjects

A debater, to exercise his powers of persuasion, needs cases to argue. To sustain his interest as well as that of his audience, he particularly needs new cases to argue. He wants subjects which relate closely to the world about him, to the society he lives in, to the problems he faces. He wants to be able to say things which haven't been said many times before.

Nevertheless, a debater can't afford to be too particular about subjects. In a well-planned competition there's a debate in any subject set before him, even if he's called on to explore the possibilities more thoroughly on some occasions than he may wish. Except perhaps in A-grade, he's unlikely to meet anything like "That Marx was a red square" or "That one plus one equals one". Usually it's a matter of asking "What does it mean?" and then "Why is this so?" or "Why is this not so?" And it's worth remembering that in competitions of standing there's no such thing as a subject which is loaded in favour of one side, though sometimes there may be one which seems so until more thought is given to it.

Debaters, once they've passed the junior stage, are recommended to speak on as many subjects, and as many varieties of subjects, as possible. Though there are basically seven kinds of subjects, as previously mentioned (Chapter 5), there are kinds within kinds. But whatever its kind, a subject still has to be interpreted and then proved by one side and disproved by the other. All subjects come down to what's very much common ground, and debaters need practice in bringing a wide range of them down to just that.

Making up subjects

Coaches and competition organisers, though making use of published subject lists, will often rightly exercise their ingenuity in setting subjects of their own. Fresh subjects come to mind regularly, and may have obvious appeal if they're of a topical nature. Controversial opinions are being continually expressed, and this should lead naturally to debate. Throughout history people have been making debatable statements, and many of these, which are often quoted in various books, are worth taking up. All sorts of arresting subjects may be devised by persons who take the trouble to know what's going on about them.

Care needs to be taken in devising a debating subject. Is its meaning clear at the particular level of debate? Is it readily debatable, or does it seem to favour one side at the expense of the other? Would the Negative be likely to encounter unreasonable difficulty in preparing a case against it? Is it within the range of experience of the teams concerned? Is it reasonably simple, or may it raise issues too complex to be dealt with in the time allowed? Is it likely to place a premium on research rather than debating skill? Is it of sufficient general interest to teams and audience? Does it offer a challenge to the debaters' skill? Is it highly controversial and therefore likely to encourage biassed statements rather than reasoned argument?

"That more men should bite dogs" has a clear meaning only to persons sufficiently well-read to know Dana's saying about what constitutes news. "That there should be more understanding on both sides of the generation gap" would be difficult to refute. "That women should promise to love, honour, but not obey" is unfair to the Affirmative because that side can't foresee in which of several directions the Negative emphasis will be placed. "That religion is out of date" isn't so much controversial as a generalisation requiring much qualification before Affirmative howls of protest would cease.

List of 700 subjects

Some subjects listed below are expressed in negative form. It's reasonable to state a subject in whatever form people are most likely to think of it. "That teachers should not strike" and "That children don't understand parents" may be taken to express a more commonly held view than if put the other way around. What matters isn't how the subject looks but what can be done with it.

The following subjects are not listed under various types, for such information isn't provided when debate subjects are set. Part of the challenge of debating lies in coming to terms with all sorts of subjects. However, listing is in groups of ten, with reasonable variety of type and difficulty in each group. In this way coaches and debaters should be able to make a varied selection of subjects to suit their needs at any level.

1   That violence has no place in entertainment.
2   That we take ourselves too seriously.
3   That we should forgive and forget.
4   That we need more time to do nothing.
5   That parents don't understand children.
6   That saying it is more effective than writing it.
7   That vandalism is an indictment of our education system.
8   That Australian men are a sorry lot.
9   That we should go where the next train goes.
10 That political philosophies are the opium of politicians.

11 That it's fun finding out.
12 That truth in advertising no longer matters.
13 That in delay there lies no plenty.
14 That a street is better than a meadow.
15 That strikes are acts of war against the community.
16 That the hand that rules the cradle rocks the world.
17 That we are being over-persuaded.
18 That we should speak our minds.
19 That job-sharing is the answer.
20 That our television channels are becoming choked with rubbish.

21 That the shorter the better.
22 That pessimism is piffle as well as poison.
23 That faded jeans are to be worn with pride.
24 That life is pulling doors marked 'Push' and pushing doors marked 'Pull'.
25 That the more the merrier.
26 That it is better to travel hopefully than to arrive.
27 That tradition is the enemy of progress.
28 That success in advertising depends on exaggeration.
29 That we should shoulder the sky.
30 That the swinger is an endangered species.

31 That Australia imitates the worst of what other countries have to offer.
32 That we should hark to Bach before we shop for pop.
33 That women are cyclonic.
34 That environmental considerations are luxuries we can no longer afford.
35 That it is easier to die in battle than to tell the truth in politics.

36   That we've got it made in the next decade.
37   That children are discriminated against.
38   That media education should form part of high-school studies.
39   That envy makes the world go round.
40   That what was good enough for our fathers is not good enough for us.

41   That government is too serious a matter to be left to politicians.
42   That sport would be better without sponsors.
43   That education should be a total experience.
44   That "no way" is no answer.
45   That girls were made to love and kiss.
46   That life is becoming too complicated.
47   That the trees are full of galahs.
48   That male chauvinists are not pigs.
49   That we should act with malice towards some.
50   That the ideals of a nation may be told from its advertisements.

51   That you should neither a borrower nor a lender be.
52   That it's no good fighting a battle you can't win.
53   That we have a duty to be provocative.
54   That the fast buck should return to the wilderness.
55   That foreign enterprise in Australia should be severely restricted.
56   That love wasn't meant to be easy.
57   That the time is out of joint.
58   That we should open our doors to refugees.
59   That high fences make good neighbours.
60   That nothing succeeds like excess.

61   That the ocker's a shocker.
62   That puritanism is paralysis.
63   That I'm-all-right-Jackery is so much quackery.
64   That scientists need to rethink their objectives.
65   That fashions are for the frivolous.
66   That the weight of the posterior is greater than the force of intellect.
67   That modern technology is changing persons into personnel.
68   That picketing is for bullies.
69   That we should look back in anger.

70   That there's a better motive than the profit motive.

71   That man is his own worst enemy.
72   That we should make hay while the sun shines.
73   That fine words butter no parsnips.
74   That the strike is no longer a fair weapon.
75   That the true success is to labour.
76   That people are much the same.
77   That dissent deserves encouragement.
78   That our education system is in need of a major overhaul.
79   That profit is not without honour.
80   That it is the old things which startle and intoxicate.

81   That now is better than later.
82   That it is more important to attack drinking than to attack smoking.
83   That publicity is a better salesman than quality.
84   That the beliefs of dogmatic persons are deliciously disputable.
85   That private morals are not for public action.
86   That woman should step down from her pedestal.
87   That ritual is ridiculous.
88   That what we need is love.
89   That a fallacy should not be left alone.
90   That one tree is worth a million rolls of newsprint.

91   That our men should wear green suits and red shirts.
92   That the Negative deserves to lose.
93   That popular newspapers shield their readers from the wider world.
94   That why and wherefore are better than therefore.
95   That there are too many babbling brooks.
96   That Rugby League should be played without a football.
97   That fame is the spur.
98   That we never get an answer.
99   That one plus one equals one.
100 That conformity is a social disease.

101 That women are not to be trusted.
102 That there is no such thing as a right to anything.
103 That work is the sustenance of noble minds.
104 That the place for knockers is outside the door.
105 That the subject isn't important.

106   That the future is not what it used to be.
107   That it pays to be suspicious.
108   That apple carts should be upset.
109   That we can't see the wood for the trees.
110   That we need more Margarets Thatching.

111   That migration is for the birds.
112   That marriage makes the man.
113   That all play and no work makes Jack a dull jerk.
114   That it's a case of the unions or the Australian people.
115   That free thought is expensive.
116   That women are the only true proletariat left.
117   That, to the man in the middle, life is a riddle.
118   That there is too much secrecy in government.
119   That the permissive society has gone too far.
120   That prophets were meant to be mocked.

121   That the majority should be in a minority.
122   That there are more snakes than ladders.
123   That, if we thought so then, we should think so still.
124   That "don't argue" is bad advice.
125   That we're a lazy lot.
126   That the carnival is over.
127   That we would rather win friends than influence people.
128   That women are a different species.
129   That we should disregard the omens and disdain the stars.
130   That we are not here for fun.

131   That we're too ready to go through on the amber.
132   That schooling hinders education.
133   That Johnny's so long at the fair.
134   That "life, be in it" is a message foreign to the Australian
      character.
135   That demonstrations are for dimwits.
136   That telling the truth is a bad habit.
137   That we should stop building freeways.
138   That there ought to be more of it.
139   That we need a children's liberation movement.
140   That the new morality is the old immorality.

141   That bludgers are beautiful.
142   That comparison breeds contempt.

143   That union membership should not be a condition of employment.

144   That we need more fanatics.

145   That television commercials are products of the counter-culture.

146   That those were the good old days.

147   That we are travelling in the wrong gear.

148   That it's afterwards that counts.

149   That there should be more women in Parliament.

150   That schooling stifles individuality.

151   That we are not sufficiently concerned with the past.

152   That technological progress has changed our lives for the worse.

153   That being lively is better than being lovely.

154   That developers are public enemies.

155   That tolerance is weakness.

156   That this is the "me" generation.

157   That, when it is not necessary to change, it is necessary not to change.

158   That if we think it matters we should shout it from the housetops.

159   That applause is a thing we eagerly seek.

160   That if you can't join them beat them.

161   That the contest is enough.

162   That we are what circumstances make us.

163   That we should keep off the grass.

164   That democracy is on the way out.

165   That we should count up to ten.

166   That, no matter how foolish the fashion, women will be slaves to it.

167   That the popular press would be dear at half the price.

168   That you never can tell.

169   That we should not neglect mumbo-jumbo.

170   That the best things are lost in victory and not in defeat.

171   That personality is on the wane.

172   That we should slow down.

173   That variety is the spice of life.

174   That women would make a better job of running the world than men have done.

175   That there's too much emphasis on getting things easily.

176 That the Joneses aren't worth keeping up with.
177 That readers of women's magazines get what they deserve.
178 That we talk about our rights when we should be talking about our responsibilities.
179 That Marx was a red square.
180 That Australia has become a paradise for the work-shy.

181 That the better the car, the better the pick-up.
182 That candour is beautiful.
183 That we are being led by the nose.
184 That poachers make the best gamekeepers.
185 That "Advance Australia Fair" is a reminder of what might have been.
186 That by their words shall ye know them.
187 That we are prisoners of a materialist society.
188 That watching television is a mental health hazard.
189 That we should turn back the clock.
190 That the media needs to show a greater sense of social responsibility.

191 That we're not doing too badly.
192 That selfishness is a social evil.
193 That putting things over keeps us in clover.
194 That the swinging singles have swung too far.
195 That we're up the creek without a paddle.
196 That today's advertising plays us for suckers.
197 That monarchical institutions improve the manners.
198 That we should shock them.
199 That what's sauce for the goose is sauce for the gander.
200 That the trend matters more than the end.

201 That the ABC has become a prisoner of the marketplace.
202 That the campaign for aboriginal land rights has gone far enough.
203 That daughters should lock up their mothers.
204 That ID cards are a no-no.
205 That macho is miserable.
206 That old hat is just as good as new hat.
207 That parents need instruction in the playing of their parts.
208 That sacred cows are fit objects for blasphemy.
209 That TV advertising is a con job.
210 That we are Hamlets putting off the moment of truth.

211 That capital and labour should have their heads knocked together.
212 That education and examinations don't go together.
213 That he who attacks the man instead of the argument is not fit for public life.
214 That if a marriage breaks down, both parties are to blame.
215 That language belongs to the people.
216 That Parliaments should be conducted with the dignity of the courts.
217 That Santa Claus is a commercial rip-off.
218 That takeovers are not in the public interest.
219 That we believe what we want to believe.
220 That woman is a foreign land.

221 That aborigines get a raw deal.
222 That bans and limitations are idiot responses.
223 That fantasy is a thing we need.
224 That if it were not for women, men would be walking around in skin suits and carrying clubs.
225 That nervous Nellies are worse than dumb Doras.
226 That old people ought to be explorers.
227 That parents should receive education vouchers to be cashed at any school of their choice.
228 That the rank and file are guardians of prejudice.
229 That saving the Franklin was a famous victory.
230 That we should declare war on cultural imperialism.

231 That caricature makes a stronger impression than character.
232 That daylight saving confuses the hens and fades the curtains.
233 That the game is more than the players.
234 That if it's good enough for teachers to strike, it's good enough for their students to do the same.
235 That a man's gotta do want a man's gotta do.
236 That omnibus-sized best-sellers fill gaps in the garbage.
237 That party politics should be thrown out of local government.
238 That semi-trailers should be banned from the highways.
239 That teachers unions have too much influence.
240 That we should go placidly amid the haste and din.

241 That the carrot is more effective than the stick.
242 That elections should not be contested in terms of rival leaders.

243   That he who hesitates is lost.
244   That if political candidates were any better we wouldn't have them, and if they were any worse we couldn't stand them.
245   That laws which protect civil liberties are a threat to society.
246   That the past is past.
247   That self-interest engages the starter.
248   That talented outsiders should be brought into government.
249   That we should heed the clamour of inequity.
250   That you do well to beware the flip side of charm.

251   That the actions of factions are no mean attractions.
252   That the barbarians are within our gates.
253   That if smokers are becoming pariahs, that's fine.
254   That Jill is as good as her master.
255   That nationalism makes world peace impossible.
256   That rapacious is the word for government.
257   That a union refusing to obey a court order should be stripped of its assets.
258   That we can do without sport, sport, sport.
259   That woman's at best a contradiction still.
260   That you have to make mistakes in order to learn from them.

261   That casinos ought to be closed.
262   That feminists screeching their heads off would gain more by subtlety.
263   That if thou wouldst a 'polly' be, yes and no are not for thee.
264   That we should shout hurrah for given names starting with X, Y and Z.
265   That on Mondays the world is flat.
266   That pastoral lands are not for Army bang-bangs.
267   That SP bookmaking should be legalised.
268   That terrorism is stupid.
269   That we don't decide our political views on reasonable grounds.
270   That 'Yes Minister' should be required viewing in the halls of government.

271   That the ABC's quest for popular relevance is clownish.
272   That the chicken-processing industry should get the bird.

273 That 'the days of philandering are over' is a slur on our menfolk.
274 That if you can't appreciate a flute concerto you need to start your education all over again.
275 That man's is the cloven hoof.
276 That Parliaments need a substantial number of Independents.
277 That the quality of life would be improved with nothing on the box one day a week.
278 That the sexual revolution has created more problems than it has solved.
279 That there can only be a worst thing since sliced bread.
280 That we need our eccentrics.

281 That barbecues at Bandywallop are all very well.
282 That electronic evangelism is pseudo-religion on the make.
283 That a file and a folder make your interlocutor bolder.
284 That if you hear a buzz-word you should swat it.
285 That manners belong to a bygone age.
286 That once a day you should run agog like hey-go-mad.
287 That peddlers of hard porn should be paid in hard labour.
288 That rare forests should not be logged.
289 That TV gives us a warped view of life.
290 That we are voyeurs peeking into one another's secrets.
291 That the ad has become a substitute for the product.
292 That the Christian Church needs a new Savonarola.
293 That girls can do anything.
294 That image has triumphed over reality.
295 That leaks are an important part of the political process.
296 That penalty rates should be abolished.
297 That the short answer is too short.
298 That there are not enough draughts in the corridors of power.
299 That we buy the brand and not the product.
300 That the woodchip industry should be clear-felled.

301 That cigarette advertising should be banned.
302 That desexing the language is silly.
303 That hedonism is our handicap.
304 That impatience is a virtue.
305 That new is better.
306 That one-day cricket is an enemy of the game.
307 That politicians don't have to be misologists.

308   That Santa shouldn't grow fat while millions starve.

309   That there is a dearth of logophiliacs.

310   That we have attained irresponsible government.

311   That basic foods should be sold at a discount.

312   That first-past-the-post voting should lose on protest.

313   That in the box should be on the box.

314   That 'Keep it stupid' is the right motto in TV advertising.

315   That marriage is an optional extra.

316   That one 'dry' is worth a dozen 'wets'.

317   That peer-group pressure merits firm resistance.

318   That ratings are the bad name of the television game.

319   That there is no such thing as a right to strike.

320   That we should bar sporting contacts with South Africa.

321   That adults have no right to have kids so wrong.

322   That a city of high-rise buildings has sold its soul.

323   That he who refuses to toe the party line is a man his party needs.

324   That in today's climate contempt charges should be brought at every opportunity.

325   That lethargy is strategy.

326   That shrinks are better shrunk.

327   That there should be no limit to trading hours.

328   That we have an obligation to be discriminating.

329   That wetlands deserve complete protection.

330   That you ought not to be congratulated.

331   That claptrap is essential to the concoction of charisma.

332   That democracy is in danger.

333   That God's police turn people off religion.

334   That in trying to be fair to aborigines we are losing perspective on the rest of us.

335   That Marxism is only a yoke.

336   That people may be properly addressed by their first names.

337   That a small group of industry unions is all that's needed.

338   That there's no fool like a young fool.

339   That when bad Australians die they are sent to Surfer's Paradise.

340   That you should wear your individuality like a badge.

341   That belief breeds bias.

342   That elegance is a thing of the past.

343 That the first Tuesday in November marks a silly tribal rite.
344 That indiscretion is a proper accompaniment of youth.
345 That levelling up makes more sense than levelling down.
346 That politicians serve nobody by politicking.
347 That reality is a nice place to visit but you wouldn't want to live there.
348 That there should be roundabout turning to left and to right.
349 That we should keep the trendies at bay.
350 That you should be different.

351 That the adversary system in our courts is due for scrapping.
352 That celibacy has no defence.
353 That Her prentice hand She tried on man, and then She made the lasses, O.
354 That jingles jangle.
355 That newspaper readers have a right not to have their heads stuffed with gossips and nonsense.
356 That quangos should go bango.
357 That the vertical thrust of our cities is a triumph of greed over taste.
358 That we are conditioned by the company we keep.
359 That worldly wisdom is worldly but not wisdom.
360 That you should be running hard and loving it.

361 That the clergy have a duty to speak up for the downtrodden.
362 That enough is too much.
363 That heroes are better without worship.
364 That infotainment subverts the news.
365 That muck-raking promotes hygiene.
366 That 'person' and 'Ms' are a bit of a fizz.
367 That smoking in public places should be prohibited.
368 That things are bleak on the box.
369 That we are what we watch.
370 That zeal should come to heel.

371 That betting is a mug's game.
372 That 'la difference' can do with fresh vive-ing.
373 That five o'clock is the time to get up.
374 That the insanity plea is crazy.
375 That the Labor party is the true conservative party.
376 That one frinstance is worth a fistful of *ipse dixits*.
377 That police booking of drivers is irrelevant to road safety.
378 That rhetoric has taken over.

379 That soapies are for dopeys.
380 That we should look after our curmudgeons.
381 That advertising is a rip-off at the consumer's expense.
382 That cricket would be better without its thick quicks.
383 That the good life has made us flabby.
384 That institutional Christianity is the first but not the second.
385 That Members of Parliament have made us as cynical as they are.
386 That pop is a case of mindless for the mindless.
387 That social acceptance is based on the wrong values.
388 That the thinker is an endangered species.
389 That we give up too easily.
390 That women's magazines display a poor attitude to women.

391 That a coat is no good if it can't be turned.
392 That environmentalists are the salt of what's left of the earth.
393 That international cricket has fallen to the level of soap opera.
394 That journalistic jargon is too jejune not to be jettisoned.
395 That liberation theology is right.
396 That one super-power is no better than the other.
397 That picketing should be punished.
398 That striking in essential industries should be out of the question.
399 That the third in line will suit me fine.
400 That we should buy Australian-made.

401 That the book of the film is worse than the film of the book.
402 That delight is found in simple things.
403 That inverted snobbery is sillier than the other sort.
404 That life mimics television.
405 That no entertainment is too bad to be true.
406 That politics is an extension of theatre.
407 That running the red is not go-ahead.
408 That thirteen is only a number.
409 That we should attach the carriages of public opinion to the locomotive of outrage.
410 That you're foolish to start something you can't finish.

411 That the Affirmative deserves to win.
412 That commercial TV promotes alien cultural values.
413 That the history of a country is the history of its ordinary people.

414 That it doesn't matter what colour the cow is so long as the milk comes out white.
415 That men are male chauvinists at heart.
416 That popular newspapers are gatherers of wheat and printers of chaff.
417 That the ugly face of unionism requires surgical treatment.
418 That we should check before we mate.
419 That women's fashions are a caricature of femininity.
420 That you should behave predictably.

421 That commune-type living is a poor alternative.
422 That flattery gets you nowhere.
423 That government isn't about right or wrong but about order or chaos.
424 That it is idolatry to take the Bible as the word of God.
425 That no position should be barred to women on account of their sex.
426 That porn requires a line to be drawn.
427 That social drinking wants rejection thinking.
428 That this is a fine country.
429 That we should be in it to win it or not in it at all.
430 That you should cross the line between 'I wish' and 'I will'.

431 That all that's wrong with winter is bad PR.
432 That booze buses should be set up outside every busy club and hotel.
433 That democracy is tied to mediocrity.
434 That it doesn't matter what the neighbours think.
435 That men are not improved by their own society.
436 That one trail bike is too many.
437 That popular is bad.
438 That the right to work should never be disputed.
439 That sodomy doesn't deserve even the faintest hint of acceptance.
440 That when is now.
441 That equality is a myth.
442 That fools need persons who won't suffer them gladly.
443 That home is where the cat is.
444 That it would be lovely to have a de-Americanised Australia.
445 That men should share the housework.
446 That practical considerations outweigh moral ones.
447 That socialism is a cure for which there is no known disease.

448 That 'thou shalt not dob' is a command for the brainless.

449 That we should pull the chain on rock groups.

450 That the world's population growth must be put into immediate reverse.

451 That communism is an enemy of the masses.

452 That football is a round-ball game.

453 That it doesn't matter whether the combs are wide or narrow so long as the sheep are shorn.

454 That life wasn't meant to be sleazy.

455 That me-too-ism is a millstone round our necks.

456 That the only worthwhile government is one of national unity.

457 That precise is preferable.

458 That striking teachers make the world safe for hypocrisy.

459 That thriving comes before wiving.

460 That we should rise to cry 'Oh frabjous day! Calloo, callay!'

461 That advertising is more concerned with imprinting than informing.

462 That born losers aren't.

463 That homosexuality is not an acceptable lifestyle in an enlightened community.

464 That the liquor industry has no sense of social responsibility.

465 That a no-strike clause should be written into every award.

466 That opinion polls are a waste of money.

467 That progress has to be kept in its place.

468 That rhetoric is the harlot of the arts.

469 That terrorists should be denied the oxygen of publicity.

470 That we should cross our bridges before we come to them.

471 That community service should be a condition of unemployment payments to young people.

472 That disguise our bondage as we will, 'tis woman, woman, rules us still.

473 That a government without a newspaper is more deplorable than a newspaper without a government.

474 That it isn't whether you believe in God but whether God believes in you.

475 That life was better before TV.

476 That preference to unionists should be hit on the head.

477 That sport is war without the shooting.

478 That 'tis not too late tomorrow to be brave.

479 That we have no right not to be what we seem.
480 That women are always striving for effect.

481 That American English isn't good enough for Australians.
482 That the company man is a monstrous creation.
483 That for every yea-sayer we have need of two nay-sayers.
484 That it's a mistake to follow your conscience unless it's going the same way as you are.
485 That no turn should be left unstoned.
486 That politics is not for honest men.
487 That sporting shooters should be turned into targets.
488 That TV trivialises all it can.
489 That we should see how the cat jumps.
490 That you should give every man your ear but few your voice.

491 That bouncers are a legitimate part of a fast bowler's repertoire.
492 That every man is a piece of the continent, a part of the main.
493 That it's a poor go when the men look like women and the women look like men.
494 That the journey is worth promoting no less than the destination.
495 That opposition by farmers to our governments is justified.
496 That pornography is the most pressing issue facing women.
497 That road haulage should give way to rail transport wherever possible.
498 That sports commentators are the limit.
499 That we should begin a no-smoking, no-drinking campaign among young people.
500 That your disdain should be made plain.
501 That complacency is the new deadly sin.
502 That dogma belongs in the doghouse.
503 That 'honi soit qui mal y pense' would lead us all a merry dance.
504 That little mates deserve support.
505 That non-negotiable is nonsensical.
506 That pragmatism is a wretched philosophy.
507 That a star wars policy is madness.
508 That to degrade language is to degrade civilisation.
509 That we should build more bridges.
510 That you wouldn't want to buy a used car from a hard seller for Jesus.

511 That any later than the King James version of the Bible is a sop to the semi-literate.

512 That compromise does better than laying it on the line.

513 That governments should be one step ahead of public opinion.

514 That it's better than riches to scratch where it itches.

515 That Members of Parliament should have a free vote in the House on every issue.

516 That State rights should give way to national interest.

517 That to stand still is not an option.

518 That we haven't enough shags sitting on rocks.

519 That we judge people by the labels we put on them.

520 That you should give way to the seven-year itch.

521 That boxing is due for axing.

522 That every million spent on roads should be matched by a million spent on railways.

523 That hot gospellers should be driven out into the cold.

524 That it's better to know a lot about a little than a little about a lot.

525 That a little of what you fancy does you good.

526 That the present so-called Lake Pedder should be drained and its wall demolished.

527 That rock is a four-letter word.

528 That the tobacco ring ought to be smashed.

529 That we watch too much television.

530 That zoo animals should not be caged.

531 That any religion which restricts women's freedom is due for reformation.

532 That compulsory unionism is an outrage.

533 That a driver failing a breath test merits a ten-year disqualification.

534 That it's dogged as does it.

535 That men who authorise the destruction of a unique wilderness are not fit for human society.

536 That opposition to imperial honours is juvenile.

537 That preservation of anything of historical value should be unquestioned.

538 That status quo-ing beats to and fro-ing.

539 That uranium should be left in the ground.

540 That we should act as if the bills were paid.

541 That country people shouldn't have to pay more for anything than city people.

542 That every person needs both yin and yang.

543 That homosexuals theft of the word 'gay' is abhorrent.
544 That it's better to say things you don't mean than to mean things you don't say.
545 That junk food should be pushed off the market.
546 That the most essential part of education is development of character.
547 That the politics of innuendo is due for diminuendo.
548 That strike-breakers are worthy of general esteem.
549 That we live in an imaginary world created by advertising agencies.
550 That women are cats in a dog's world.
551 That broad acres do not guarantee broad minds.
552 That for young people low pay beats no pay.
553 That it's fine walking on eggshells.
554 That kitsch should be laughed out of existence.
555 That lobbyists should be combed out.
556 That optional preferential voting should lose the option.
557 That the price is wrong.
558 That romance is a steam train.
559 That to-ing has the edge on fro-ing.
560 That we were sold a metric pup.
561 That the American impact on Western civilisation has been disastrous.
562 That confession is bad for the soul.
563 That greenies are great.
564 That it's fine to be a ferro-equinophile.
565 That the microcosm we see becomes the macrocosm that mirrors us.
566 That a private conscience is a public nuisance.
567 That style's the thing.
568 That television is chewing-gum for the eyes.
569 That we're becoming too physical.
570 That you should keep your tents apart and your hearts together.

571 That consensus is the abandonment of principle.
572 That drop-outs should be denied the dole.
573 That it's harder for girls.
574 That logorrhoea should be regarded as a notifiable disease.
575 That others do it is a good reason for not doing it.
576 That pressure groups are out of place in a democracy.
577 That the Vicar of Bray has been foully maligned.
578 That we should deal with the assassins of silence.

579 That women are more often realists than men.

580 That we should let the radials stray from the arterials.

581 That as a man fantasies so is he.

582 That a bucketful of butts should be a fixture on every tobacco executive's desk.

583 That free tertiary education is absurd.

584 That it's jam yesterday, jam tomorrow, but never jam today.

585 That non-parole periods should not be reduced.

586 That politics should be kept out of sport.

587 That the rugby codes should be phased out in favour of soccer and Australian football.

588 That speech writers should be denied writing materials.

589 That we're being brainwashed by consumerism.

590 That yuppies only think they're uppies.

591 That consumers are being taken for a ride.

592 That every shopping district should have its pedestrian mall.

593 That how a message is conveyed is more important than the message.

594 That it's nice to be important, but more important to be nice.

595 That men are deceivers ever.

596 That 'ought' ought not, and 'ought not' ought not.

597 That private schools warrant increased public funds.

598 That the sugar and salt content of processed foods should be reduced almost to nothing.

599 That tolls on public roads and bridges should be abolished.

600 That we've been there, done that.

601 That the Asianisation of Australia is inevitable.

602 That controversial statements deserve a warm welcome.

603 That drug pushers should get life.

604 That it's the Church's place to attack abuses of power.

605 That the middle class is the muddled class.

606 That privatisation is an ugly word but the idea is a good one.

607 That a summit is summat.

608 That tomorrow never comes.

609 That we need bobbies on the beat.

610 That women should set an example to men by neither smoking nor drinking.

611 That BUGA-UP deserves support.
612 That full Marx earns no marks.
613 That governments should get out of gambling.
614 That it's no good having a secret if you make a secret of it.
615 That militant teachers are a blot on our education system.
616 That the problem isn't finding the answers but finding the questions.
617 That Queensland is another country.
618 That Sunday's too far away.
619 That too much spoils the flavour.
620 That we need our ginger groups.
621 That the convention industry wears a tourist hat and a silly face.
622 That everyone needs a stock of prejudices.
623 That how parents turn out is the responsibility of their children.
624 That juries should be allowed to give majority verdicts.
625 That morality cannot be expected in international affairs.
626 That our cities are going down the gurgle hole.
627 That proclivities offer more excitement than propensities.
628 That the ruling passion conquers reason still.
629 That trade unions have outlived their usefulness.
630 That we should rid our nation of Yankee influence.

631 That Australian education is a disastrous smorgasbord.
632 That cricket is no longer the grand old game.
633 That it's not the driver but the caravanserai.
634 That the long way round is the best way home.
635 That nostalgia puts the present in focus.
636 That promoters of rock concerts are corrupters of youth.
637 That swinging voters are the harlots of politics.
638 That travel makes you appreciate the joys of staying home.
639 That we need more people of a certain grandeur.
640 That the workers have nothing to lose but the chains put on them by those who say they have nothing to lose but their chains.
641 That buying on the never-never is anything but very clever.
642 That drivers' licences should be restricted to persons who have passed an advanced driving test.
643 That it's not what you do but how you do it.
644 That losing has become a dirty word.

645 That not without reason do we speak of the common man.
646 That the public service is full of Bristows, with not a Fudge in sight.
647 That small business should be of more concern to governments than big business.
648 That use of performing animals in entertainment ought to be banned.
649 That we need more elitists.
650 That you should never give a sucker an even break.
651 That examinations are a good preparation for life.
652 That the function of boards is to justify their existence.
653 That growing up is one hiccup after another.
654 That it's silly to go crook on a Monday.
655 That nothing beats doing nothing.
656 That public opinion is the organised ignorance of the community.
657 That Rugby League is a mindless and violent exercise performed by macho clones.
658 That a tradition of party loyalty is undesirable.
659 That you should never do today what you can put off till tomorrow.
660 That you should pick yourself off, dust yourself down, and start all over again.

661 That Australians have lost their pioneering spirit.
662 That creationism threatens reason.
663 That it's there in your handwriting.
664 That love is wasted on the young.
665 That our nationalism goes no deeper than waving an Australian flag.
666 That pupils should be able to sue their teachers for incompetence.
667 That 'Vote 1 for charisma' is splendid advice.
668 That we should let sleeping dogs lie.
669 That women are still treated as the second sex.
670 That you should never trust a man with a centre parting.

671 That a clutch of Cassandras is preferable to a plethora of Pollyannas.
672 That fundamentalism is opposed to the spirit of religion.
673 That how you doodle shows what sort of person you are.
674 That it's not what you say but how you say it.
675 That our social conscience needs prodding into wakefulness.

676 That public service numbers should be put on the downhill run.
677 That rock is ripe for ridicule.
678 That socialised medicine is a weed to be pulled out before it takes hold.
679 That we need more women flexing their political muscles.
680 That you should refuse to buy eggs laid by battery hens.

681 That the duty of an Opposition is to provide it.
682 That the future is woman.
683 That humanity is enslaved to corporate command.
684 That the lowest common denominator should be sent back to the schoolroom.
685 That militant unionism is one of the social diseases.
686 That our young folk should be trained to pass up the weeds for the flowers.
687 That the purpose of advertising is to trick people into accepting what they get.
688 That synthetic celebrities are the personification of our hollow dreams.
689 That trade unions should aim to extend the social and cultural horizons of their members.
690 That we should love the game beyond the prize.

691 That a cynic is a realist by another name.
692 That excellence is the goal to aim at.
693 That girls should refuse to conform to their stereotypes.
694 That it's us or them.
695 That nothing so needs reforming as other people's habits.
696 That pussyfooting is favoured only for felines.
697 That the right road is the one that goes uphill.
698 That the trouble with children is adults.
699 That the writing is on the wall.
700 That you shouldn't do only one thing at a time.